GOD'S

SELF-CONTROL

Fruit

WALKING THROUGH THE FIELDS OF GRACE AND MERCY IN BLOOM

COMPILED BY ANGELA R. EDWARDS

God's Self-Control Fruit:
WALKING THROUGH THE FIELDS OF GRACE AND MERCY IN BLOOM

Compiled By:
Angela R. Edwards

With Contributions By
(in order of appearance):
Rev. Dr. Marilyn E. Porter
Laurie Benoit
Angela Edwards
Keywana Wright-Jones
Reyna Harris-Goynes
Precious Damas
Tosha R. Dearbone
Dr. Joanne B. Lewis
Katina Rice-Davis
Simone Holyfield
Marlowe R. Scott
Maresa Roach
Tiffany Pope
Dr. Sonya Alise McKinzie
Dr. Cheryl Kehl

RsP.
Redemption's Story
Publishing, LLC

Redemption's Story Publishing, LLC, Harlem, GA (USA)

God's Self-Control Fruit:
Walking Through the Fields of Grace and Mercy in Bloom

Copyright © 2025
Angela R. Edwards

ISBN 13: 978-1-948853-90-3
Library of Congress Control Number: 2025948100
Printed in the U.S.A.

Scripture references are used with permission from Zondervan via Biblegateway.com. Public Domain.

For information and bulk ordering, contact:
Redemption's Story Publishing, LLC
Angela Edwards, CEO
P.O. Box 639
Harlem, GA 30814
RedemptionsStoryPublishing2020@gmail.com

Dedication

Thank you, dear readers,
for journeying with us through these pages. Your
engagement inspires every word written. May this
book resonate deeply, sparking reflection and growth.
We hope it encourages you to embrace your own path
with courage, faith, and the transformative power of
self-control.

Acknowledgments

First, I give all honor and glory to my **Heavenly Father** for His guidance in putting this "God's Fruit" series together. From the beginning, He touched the hearts of each author while granting them the strength to pen remarkable truths that have continually blessed others.

To my Husband, **James Edwards**: As always, I thank you for and appreciate your love and patience as I spent numerous hours piecing together each project in the series. You remain nothing short of amazing throughout the process. I love you beyond mere words.

To my Foreword writer, **Rev. Dr. Marilyn E. Porter**: Thank you, MURL, for the spiritual insight you have provided in every single book in the "God's Fruit" series. I have no doubt you fulfilled your God-given assignment with each word you wrote. You have a way of "bringing it" that is unmatched. I love you, girl!

To my Mother, **Marlowe R. Scott**: Not many know the behind-the-scenes work you do as we work to bring these projects to life. Your keen eye and support at every turn cannot be understated. You are amazing, and I'm grateful for the lessons and expertise you've taught me throughout the years. I love you, Mommy, and pray God's continued blessings on your life.

Last but not least, to the Contributing Authors (in no particular order)—**Sonya McKinzie, Cheryl Kehl, Keywana Wright-Jones, Marlowe Scott, Laurie Benoit, Katina Rice-Davis, Tosha Dearbone, Tiffany Pope,**

Joanne B. Lewis, Maresa Roach, Precious Damas, Simone Holyfield, and Reyna Harris-Goynes: Ladies, thank you ALL for saying YES when others stepped to the side. They made room for YOUR gifts, and I am grateful for each of you and your commitment to see this project through to the end. I love you all! May you be BLESSED beyond measure as your stories reach those who need it most.

Foreword by Rev. Dr. Marilyn E. Porter

According to Google.com (2025), *"self-control involves managing impulses and resisting urges to act on them immediately, especially when those actions might be detrimental to long-term well-being or goals."*

The **biblical** reference to self-control refers to *"temperance; the inner strength and moderation to master one's desires, passions, and actions, particularly in the face of temptation and provocation."*

So, it appears that no matter how you cut it, self-control requires one to have knowledge of *self*. Self, meaning you, I, me, them, us, and they. Yes, we have a responsibility here to be aware of (self), truthful about (self), and humble before God (The Manufacture of self) to even begin to master how to control or contain. Self-control does not require one to become someone else. No. It requires a far greater task than becoming; it requires us to master the moments that we sit in on a day-to-day basis. Before becoming new, while yet on the hamster wheel, self-control lives in the processes and is an extension of how we love and care for *self*.

King David serves as a notable biblical example of self-control and its processes. Let's examine a moment when he lacked self-control, as seen when he visited the palace's roof while Uriah's wife was bathing in the evening. The Word of God (2 Samuel 11:1-5) states:

"In the spring, at the time when kings go off to war, David sent Joab out with the king's men and the whole Israelite

army. They destroyed the Ammonites and besieged Rabbah. But David remained in Jerusalem. One evening, David got up from his bed and walked around on the roof of the palace. From the roof, he saw a woman bathing. The woman was very beautiful, and David sent someone to find out about her. The man said, 'She is Bathsheba, the daughter of Eliam and the wife of Uriah the Hittite.' Then David sent messengers to get her. She came to him, and he slept with her. (Now, she was purifying herself from her monthly uncleanness.) Then she went back home. The woman conceived and sent word to David, saying, 'I am pregnant.'"

I will give you the pleasure of reading the remainder of that chapter and discovering the outcome of the King's inability to control his passions.

I mentioned David's **lack** of self-control first—the moment after he had already become the king. Next, I will show you a moment when this same man, David, exercised complete self-control. Follow me into the cave. The Word of God (1 Samuel 24:3-6) states:

"He came to the sheep pens along the way; a cave was there, and Saul went in to relieve himself. David and his men were far back in the cave. The men said, 'This is the day the LORD spoke of when He said to you, 'I will give your enemy into your hands for you to deal with as you wish.' Then David crept up unnoticed and cut off a corner of Saul's robe. Afterward, David was conscience-stricken for having cut off a corner of his robe. He said to his men, 'The LORD forbid that I should do such a thing to my master, the LORD's anointed, or lay my hand on him; for he is the anointed of the LORD.'"

Here, we observe a younger David—not yet King David—exercising remarkable self-control. He suppresses the urge to seek revenge on a man who, just hours earlier, was trying to kill him. David quiets the loud desire for retaliation and honors God by sparing Saul's life. However, notice how he easily maintained self-control when **another's** life was at stake. Yet, he arranged a hit on Bathsheba's husband and didn't consider his **own** safety in the process.

As I said before, self-control begins with how we love and care for *self*!

The Father does not limit us to imprison us. Instead, He offers the choice of self-control as a way to freely show love and gratitude to Him, allowing us to honor His creation of everything—including YOU, my friend. Ultimately, self-control is yet another way God places bumpers in the road to protect us.

To the incredible woman of God who has guided this remarkable series of books on the Fruit of the Spirit: Thank you for exercising the self-control—the discipline—to stay committed to completing this literary journey. Thanks, Ang, for seeing us all through until the end.

Rev. Dr. Marilyn E. Porter, MSML, CPC, CBC
Spiritual Life Coach, Prophetic Strategist & Visionary Leader
Founder: The Pink Pulpit | Preachers In Sneakers | This
Woman's Worth, Inc.
www.marilyneporter.com

Introduction

Self-control is one of the most profound and difficult virtues to develop in human life. Deeply rooted in spiritual tradition and personal discipline, it is a result not only of human effort but also of divine grace. This collection, "God's Self-Control Fruit: Walking Through the Fields of Grace and Mercy in Bloom," gathers a variety of voices—each sharing unique journeys marked by struggle, resilience, and transformation through the lens of self-control as a Fruit of the Spirit.

At its core, this work examines self-control as a vital part of spiritual growth and personal empowerment. It is not just about restraining or suppressing desires, but about mastering oneself in the face of temptation, adversity, and emotional upheaval. The contributors use biblical stories, personal testimonies, and real-life experiences to demonstrate how self-control is closely connected to self-awareness, love, and faith. From the biblical example of King David's moments of failure and restraint to modern stories of overcoming addiction, trauma, and relationship struggles, the document highlights that self-control is both a divine gift and a daily practice.

The contributors collectively argue that self-control is essential to living a life aligned with God's purpose. It helps believers resist harmful impulses, find peace amid chaos, and build healthy relationships rooted in truth and grace. The stories show that self-control often develops through hardship—whether fighting addiction, enduring abuse, coping with grief, or dealing with the complexities of co-parenting and personal loss. However, amid these challenges, self-control becomes a source of healing and strength, demonstrating the transformative power of God's Spirit at work within.

Moreover, this book highlights that self-control is closely linked to self-love and self-care. It challenges the misconception that self-control means becoming someone else or suppressing your true self. Instead, it encourages readers to see self-control as an act of loving oneself as God's creation—honoring the body, mind, and spirit. The spiritual practice of self-control is shown as a protective and freeing force, helping us face life's challenges with wisdom, patience, and grace.

This compilation also emphasizes practical aspects of self-control, including setting boundaries, managing emotions, and stewarding time and resources in accordance with divine priorities. The contributors share insights on how self-control relates to mental health, addiction recovery, and emotional regulation, providing readers with both inspiration and actionable advice.

In summary, this work is a heartfelt invitation to explore the fields of grace and mercy, cultivating self-control not as a burden but as a blossoming fruit of the Spirit. It urges readers to see the sacredness of self-mastery, the power of truth-telling, and the hope that comes from surrendering to God's transformative love.

Through these pages, one finds that self-control isn't the absence of struggle but the presence of divine strength guiding every step toward freedom, healing, and spiritual growth.

Table of Contents

Dedication vi

Acknowledgments vii

Foreword by Rev. Dr. Marilyn E. Porter ix

Introduction xiii

Laurie Benoit.. 1

    Pain… Suffering… Self-Control… Release

Angela R. Edwards... 7

    Self-Control: The Weight of Restraint

Keywana Wright-Jones 20

    A Believer's Life Necessitates Self-Control

Reyna Harris-Goynes 23

    A Mother to "All of Them"

Precious Damas 29

    The Power of the Pause

Tosha R. Dearbone 37

    My Fruit Matters

Dr. Joanne B. Lewis 44

    Healing from Within

Katina Rice-Davis 49

    The Strength Within

Simone Holyfield 56

    Through the Shadows to the Light

Marlowe R. Scott 66

   Restraining and Gaining

Maresa Roach 76

   Single, Saved, and Satisfied in Surrender!

Tiffany Pope 84

   How Chaos Developed Discipline

Dr. Sonya Alise McKinzie 91

   Cultivating the Spirit in the Heat of Co-Parenting

Dr. Cheryl Kehl 98

   Time Management as a Spiritual Discipline

Afterword.. 106

Self-Control—It's in God's Word 108

Laurie Benoit

Dedication: To everyone who wakes up each day and fights silent battles… Who chooses restraint when their pain demands to be released. Who have stumbled, fallen, and clawed their way back from the edge more times than they want to admit. **This is for you.**

Bio: Laurie Benoit is an author and survivor who has experienced both beauty and chaos in life. After years of abuse, she has emerged with resilience, courage, and compassion. Her mission is to raise awareness about the impact of abuse, support others in their healing process, advocate for change, and remind others that they are not alone on their journey. Laurie's work blends the transformative power of words with impactful creativity and the peaceful energy of nature. Her book, *The Transformative Power of "The Word,"* is a hauntingly moving testament to her journey of healing and inspiration. Connect with Laurie at facebook.com/onceawakened.

Pain... Suffering... Self-Control... Release

Self-control (noun): *The ability to control one's emotions and desires, especially in difficult situations.* (Oxford Languages)

Speaking from experience, in the face of adversity, self-control is often a lesson learned through repetition. From a young age, I understood that controlling my feelings and thoughts wasn't optional; it was essential for my safety. But in quiet moments of reflection, I wonder: Was I truly in control, or was I simply silenced?

Admittedly, grace hasn't always gone hand in hand with my restraint. There have been many times when I failed to maintain self-control, and I bear the burden of those moments in buried pain, lingering guilt, and deep remorse for the hurt I caused.

Rage, not anger. All-out rage. Darkness... deep, seething, unrelenting darkness. That's where I discovered that my control had slipped. To this day, I fully accept responsibility for those extreme actions and refuse to give myself "forgiveness," because they serve as stark reminders of my humanity and the abuse I have endured over the years. In many ways, that is why I've carried so much self-hatred, harming others as I acted out the pain that was once inflicted on me, sometimes terribly. Rage was never the fire; it was the residual kindling of soaked grief.

Self-Control

Nearly 40 years have passed since my most chaotic episodes, but my vow remains unshaken. I will never lose control again... at least not if I can help it. If I must bear wrath,

2

I'd rather do so alone than harm another soul. Maybe that's why I've put up with so much from others—the deeply ingrained belief from childhood that I deserved it. It was a lesson I learned as a child... but was it embedded even deeper? The idea that I was worthless, unworthy of kindness, and the lowest of the low. After all, if I didn't truly deserve it, why have I gone through so much suffering in just one lifetime?

People often give endless justifications for cruelty and abuse, but in all my years, I've learned this: There is never a reason that justifies hurting others. Similarly, for the harm I've caused, I make no excuses. I made those choices, and I firmly believe that "forgiveness" is not mine to claim for those moments.

Years of generational trauma and systemic neglect left me overwhelmed with outrage. Bullying in school and abuse in foster care layered additional burdens I was already struggling to carry. When the system meant to support me became indifferent, my anger ignited. In retaliation, I acted out— actions I have regretted ever since. They served as harsh lessons and painful reminders of why self-control is important.

I was enraged towards others, and then inward rage took hold. In my pain of hurting others, I have more than once tried to put an end to my own demise.

But emotional regulation hasn't been the only area where my self-control has been tested.

Addiction

Addiction was my escape, my crutch. I began smoking cigarettes at eight years old. Then, in my teens, I turned to alcohol and drugs, which carried me well into adulthood, all while trying to bury what felt unbearable.

But coping with addiction also has its own dark side.

Did it help? Cigarettes dulled the edges of my rage at times but never erased its source. I don't want to sensationalize tobacco use, but it was a crutch for more than just my rage—it was well-suited to handle my various stressors in life. From the aches of stress, pain, anger, financial worries, and poverty, they were more present than any other addiction. Alcohol and drugs offered only fleeting relief, which often made my loss of control worse.

I got stuck in a vicious cycle of numbing the pain, falling apart, and drowning in debt, regret, and self-loathing. Professionals often labeled me without understanding my full situation, when all I really needed was relief from my companions: pain and anger.

And yet, over the course of my life, it would be many years before I was reminded of and recognized the gift of release.

Eventually, I hit rock bottom. Again. And again. Each time, it was deeper. Each time, it was harder. Clawing my way out became a full-time endeavor... one minute, one hour, one day, and one task at a time. I held myself together, not because I felt strong, but because falling apart always cost me so much more.

Letting go of the habits that kept me trapped and stagnant started with alcohol. I had no control when I drank. I couldn't even look at myself in the mirror because I despised who I'd become. And for me, these words aren't used lightly. **Despise. Hate.** They run deep.

Gradually, as I released each addiction, I regained pieces of control—pieces of myself and the person I am. The person I can only ever aspire to be.

But my journey didn't end there, either.

The Workplace

New battlefields. New lessons. Having endured the abuse I have, workplace bullying presented fresh challenges. Power dynamics, subtle cruelty, and institutional indifference tested my self-control once again. And again, I didn't always navigate those trials with grace. Eventually, those experiences left me without a career, forcing me to change course and head in completely new directions.

Rock bottom has never truly been the end. It's usually been the silence before I find my voice. And yes, I still hold anger toward those forced-fed changes, but I am still growing... still healing. Thankfully, my understanding of employment laws has offered some protection, though, admittedly, it rarely leads to a satisfying resolution. Instead, it has pushed me to adapt and change.

Today

This year, 2025, has brought fresh trials and a new phase: menopause.

The "pre-golden years" don't feel so golden when your emotions spiral out of control and darkness returns... like day turning into night.

My journey toward menopause started early, after I had a total hysterectomy before turning forty. But this year has been especially challenging. *Wild emotions. Depression without an apparent reason. Isolation.* No crutches available. No medical support.

During the COVID pandemic, I experienced medical abuse that left me with PTSD, and another incident afterward that destroyed my confidence in a system we should be able to trust as we approach those golden years. In fact, asking for help now feels insurmountable. This is another system that has failed me, and so I need time to heal from this as well.

And so... again my gift lies dormant... until this moment... as I try once more to hold on to self-control.

Reflection

In truth, every chapter of my story reinforces this truth: We can't rewrite the past, but it can shape us. Self-control isn't easy. It's not innate. It's forged through adversity, pain, and choice. I choose to keep learning, growing, and honoring the strength it takes to face rage, hurt, and darkness without letting them define me.

In learning self-control, I discovered that release isn't about letting go of pain; it's about recognizing that I can choose peace. *And maybe, for the first time, peace isn't just the absence of pain... but the return of my voice, unburdened.*

Angela R. Edwards

Dedication: My story is dedicated to my mother, Marlowe R. Scott. Throughout the 50+ years that I have been on this earth, she has demonstrated time and again that self-control includes taming the tongue, but not to the degree that we should remain silent when being harmed or disrespected. Thank you, Mom, for being a beacon of light in my life today and always.

Bio: Angela R. Edwards is the Chief Editorial Director of Pearly Gates Publishing and Redemption's Story Publishing—two small press Christian publishing houses located in Georgia. She is the wife of James Edwards, a mother of six in a blended family, and grandmother of twenty-six. Angela loves life to the fullest, never taking a day for granted, and thanks God for every breath He allows her to take. Her motto is, *"Not today, Satan... and tomorrow isn't looking too good for you either!"*

Self-Control: The Weight of Restraint

There's something haunting about the sound of keys fumbling at the door at 3:00 a.m. That singular moment—the space between the first rattle and when the door finally swings open—holds infinite dread. I used to think that my silence was a sign of strength. I now understand it was fear masquerading as love.

"Nick" and I met one night at a nightclub while I was out with a friend. The moment I saw him, I couldn't help but notice him. He was tall, dark, and handsome, with a bright smile that lit up the dimly lit room. Our eyes met across the crowded dance floor, and the chemistry was immediate and electric. We spent that night dancing and talking over the pulsing music. By closing time, we were inseparable. Our connection was intense from the start—the kind where you stayed up until dawn discussing dreams and disappointments in the same breath. Within weeks, our relationship accelerated with the urgency of two people who believed they'd found something rare and precious.

What I didn't realize then—what I couldn't have known without him telling me—was that Nick had already formed a buddy-buddy relationship with cocaine. He later told me it started occasionally, just something to get him through long days at whatever construction site he was working at that month. He was, after all, a "Jack of all trades," skilled with his hands but restless in spirit. By the time we decided to move in together, what had been powder had evolved into crack, and what was once occasional had become essential.

"Be completely humble and gentle; be patient, bearing with one another in love." Ephesians 4:2 became my silent

mantra, though I hadn't fully grasped what "bearing with" actually looked like early on in our relationship. My understanding is entirely different now.

The First Discovery

I found the crack pipe three months after we moved in together, tucked inside a toolbox beneath a tangle of measuring tapes and levels. I sat on our bed, the evidence of Nick's secret life cold in my palm, and waited for him to come home. When he finally walked through the door, I could tell immediately that he wasn't in his right mind. His pupils were dilated, and his movements were too precise, as if he were overcompensating for his internal chaos. The words I had rehearsed evaporated. Instead of confronting him, I heard myself say, "I was thinking we could order Chinese food for dinner."

The pipe stayed hidden in my nightstand drawer. That evening, we had dinner and talked about his newest job opportunity as if nothing had changed... as if the foundation of our relationship hadn't just collapsed beneath us.

Later that night, while Nick slept beside me, I silently wept, wondering why I couldn't bring myself to speak the truth. Was it love? Fear? Or something more selfish, like the terror of confronting his addiction and what it would mean for us?

"Have I not commanded you? Be strong and courageous. Do not be afraid, do not be discouraged, for the Lord your God will be with you wherever you go." Joshua 1:9 seemed to whisper from the pages of my bedside Bible, but courage felt impossibly distant.

The Pattern Emerges

What followed was a dance of avoidance that lasted nearly seven years. Nick would work diligently at a new construction job, impressing foremen with his versatility and quick learning. But "the pattern" became painfully predictable. He'd work just long enough to receive his first paycheck, then disappear for days. The money that should have helped stabilize our finances vanished with him, leaving behind elaborate stories about "helping friends in need" or "opportunities too good to pass up."

"This new foreman really recognizes my potential," he'd say upon returning, his eyes never quite meeting mine. "I'm going to stick with this one. I promise. We're starting a big project next week. Blah, blah, blah."

I nodded, swallowing the words that threatened to spill out: *I know what you're doing. I know where the money's going. I know your promises are as empty as the rooms you sometimes construct.*

Each time I chose silence, believing somehow that my restraint was an act of love rather than cowardice. I told myself I was giving him space to find his way back, that confrontation would only push him further into his addiction. In reality, my silence was becoming complicity.

"Carry each other's burdens, and in this way, you will fulfill the law of Christ." Galatians 6:2 offered guidance, but I was carrying Nick's secrets rather than his burdens, enabling him rather than helping.

The Night Everything Changed

The breaking point came on what should have been a celebration. Nick had managed to keep a roofing job for nearly three months—a record in our time together. His boss even mentioned potential crew leadership if Nick continued his reliable work. I had planned a small dinner party with family and friends, cooking his favorite dishes and feeling hopeful that perhaps this time would be different.

As evening approached and guests began arriving, Nick was nowhere to be found. My calls went straight to voicemail. I made excuses for him—he's picking up some things for the party, he's finishing a last-minute job, he's stuck in traffic—each lie easier to tell than the last after so much practice. By midnight, the party guests had awkwardly departed, leaving behind half-eaten food and concerned glances. I sat alone on our couch, surrounded by celebration decorations that now seemed to mock me, when the phone rang.

"Angela?" an unfamiliar voice asked. "This is Mercy Hospital. We have Nick here. He's experienced what appears to be an overdose..."

The world shrank to a single moment of awareness. I remember little of the drive to the hospital, only the overwhelming sense of realization: my silence—my self-control—had nearly cost Nick his life.

In the sterile brightness of the hospital room, watching the shallow rise and fall of Nick's chest, something inside me finally broke open. When his eyes eventually fluttered open, I didn't offer comfort or pretend everything would be fine.

"I've known about the crack for a while now," I said, my voice steady despite the tears streaming down my face. "I found your pipe. I watched the money from nearly every paycheck disappear along with you. I've pretended to believe every story. And I said nothing because I was afraid of losing you. But my silence has been destroying us both."

Nick's face crumpled, not with anger but with something akin to relief. "I've been waiting," he whispered hoarsely. "Every day, I've been waiting for you to say something, to make me stop pretending."

That night signaled the start of honest communication between us. It wasn't gentle or easy, but it was genuine in a way nothing had been for years.

"Therefore, having put away falsehood, let each one of you speak the truth with his neighbor, for we are members one of another." Ephesians 4:25 suddenly made perfect sense! Our silence had kept us apart when only the truth could bring us together.

The Long Recovery

The months that followed were some of the most difficult of my life. Nick agreed to start an outpatient rehab program, and I committed to both individual and couples therapy. We discovered that my silence—what I had justified as self-control and patience—was actually a form of self-protection that ultimately protected neither of us.

"Your silence enabled my addiction," Nick told me during a particularly difficult therapy session. "Every time you didn't confront me about disappearing with my paycheck, I took it as permission to continue. I told myself that if it were that bad, you would've said something."

His words stung with truth. My therapist helped me understand that what I had called self-control—biting my tongue, swallowing my fears, and hiding my knowledge of his addiction—wasn't restraint but avoidance. True self-control would have meant facing brutal truths and having painful conversations rather than retreating into silent complicity.

"For God has not given us a spirit of fear, but of power and of love and of a sound mind." 2 Timothy 1:7 became more than just a comfort; it also presented a challenge. What does it truly mean to live with power, love, and soundness of mind in the face of addiction?

For me, it meant learning to speak uncomfortable truths out loud. It meant establishing boundaries that felt frightening in their firmness. It meant being ready to risk the relationship itself for the sake of a genuine connection.

For Nick, recovery meant not just staying sober but also taking responsibility. The man who had concealed himself behind complicated lies started practicing radical honesty, even when—especially when—the truth was unflattering.

"I'm having cravings today," he would tell me, his voice shaking but determined. "Not acting on them, but they're there, and I wanted you to know."

Those moments of vulnerability, though painful for both of us, fostered something we had never truly experienced before: authentic intimacy based on honesty rather than comfort.

"The truth will set you free." John 8:32 wasn't just spiritual wisdom but practical reality, as we found that honesty, no matter how hard, made room for healing.

The Isolation Ends

One of the most painful aspects of loving someone with an addiction was the isolation. For years, I carried Nick's secret like a heavy stone, unable to share my fears with family or friends. I became an expert at canceling plans whenever Nick was in crisis, making excuses for why we couldn't make rent again, and hiding the financial strain of his habit.

"I felt so alone," I admitted to the therapist. "Like I was the only thing standing between Nick and complete destruction, but I couldn't tell anyone why I was so exhausted all the time."

As part of our healing process, we slowly started sharing our story with trusted family and friends. Their responses varied—some with judgment, others with immense support—but simply speaking our truth out loud lifted a huge burden.

Our small community rallied around us—friends who would check in during tough anniversaries or triggers, and family members who learned about addiction so they could understand instead of judge. The isolation that had characterized much of our relationship gradually gave way to connection.

"Two are better than one, because they have a good return for their labor. If either of them falls down, one can help the other up. But pity anyone who falls and has no one to help them up." Ecclesiastes 4:9-10 reminds us that we were never meant to bear such heavy burdens alone.

Finding My Voice

Perhaps the most significant change was within myself. The woman who had swallowed her words for years out of fear began to trust her own voice. I realized that speaking truth wasn't cruel but necessary, and that boundaries weren't rejection but love at its most mature form.

In therapy, I uncovered childhood patterns that taught me to equate peacekeeping with love and to believe my needs mattered less than maintaining harmony. As I challenged these beliefs, my relationship with Nick changed.

"I need to know where you are," I would say. "Not because I don't trust you, but because I deserve consideration," or "If you take this construction job, we need a plan for payday. That's been a trigger before, so we need to address it directly."

Each boundary calmly yet firmly set was an act of love—for Nick, for me, and for the relationship we were working to rebuild.

"Let your conversation be always full of grace, seasoned with salt, so that you may know how to answer everyone." Colossians 4:6 guided my new approach to communication. Be truthful but kind, clear but compassionate.

The Ongoing Battle

Nick's struggle with addiction continued to be a perilous journey. There were periods of solid recovery where he would maintain steady work, contribute to the household, and actively participate in his support group. During those times, I caught glimpses of the man I had fallen in love with—creative, warm, quick to laugh, and talented with his hands.

Then, there would be setbacks—a former using buddy offering him work on a job site, the stress of a particularly demanding foreman, or sometimes no discernible trigger at all. The relapses became less frequent and shorter in duration as the years passed, but they never entirely disappeared.

Through everything, I stayed committed to honesty. I stopped pretending not to see the signs. I stopped making excuses to family, friends, or employers. I stopped keeping his secrets. "I love you," I would tell him during hard times, "but I won't lie for you anymore. And I won't watch you destroy yourself."

Sometimes, those boundaries caused temporary separations. Other times, they led to difficult conversations with his family. Always, they involved choosing truth over comfort, reality over illusion.

"The Lord is close to the brokenhearted and saves those who are crushed in spirit." Psalm 34:18 became my comfort during those dark times, a reminder that brokenness was not a sign of abandonment.

What Remains

It's been over twenty-five years since those tumultuous years with Nick. Reflecting on the passing of time brings both understanding and sadness. The patterns we formed—both destructive and healing—shaped not just our relationship but also the people we became.

Nick struggled with addiction for many years after our relationship ended. There were times of recovery that gave hope to everyone who loved him—moments when his natural charm and talent reappeared, making it seem like the demons had finally been defeated. He continued working construction jobs with increasing stability, sometimes even taking on small, independent projects that showcased his remarkable craftsmanship.

But addiction is a relentless adversary. Five years ago, I got the call I had both feared and, in some part of my heart, anticipated. Nick had died, his body finally succumbing to the substance that had taken so much of his life.

I didn't attend the memorial service. After all, what could I have said that would have captured the Nick I knew—brilliant and broken, loving and destructive, fighting for sobriety even as he surrendered to cravings? How could I explain that loving him had taught me the hardest but most valuable lesson of my life: that true love speaks truth, even when it hurts? My years with Nick were defined by learning when silence acted as healing and when it caused destruction. I had learned, painfully and imperfectly, the difference between self-control and self-silencing.

"Love does not delight in evil but rejoices with the truth." 1 Corinthians 13:6 has become the foundation of my understanding of love—not the comfortable, conflict-avoiding silence I once mistook for patience, but the brave, clear-eyed truth-telling that values the beloved's wholeness above temporary peace.

Nick's life ended too soon, claimed by the very demon he fought so valiantly. But his struggle—and my journey alongside

17

him—changed my understanding of what it truly means to love someone caught in addiction's grip. Sometimes, the most loving act is the hardest: breaking the silence that shields addiction from consequences, speaking painful truths, and choosing long-term healing over short-term peace.

I still mourn for Nick—for the man he was at his best, for the life addiction took from him, and for all the beauty his hands could have created if they hadn't been so often busy embracing the next high. But I am also grateful for what our broken love taught me about courage, about finding my voice, and about loving in a way that values truth more than comfort.

"He will wipe every tear from their eyes. There will be no more death or mourning or crying or pain, for the old order of things has passed away." Revelation 21:4 provides comfort that, for Nick at least, the battle is finally over.

Loving Through the Silence: A Reflection

In the aftermath of loving someone consumed by addiction, I've come to understand that true strength lies not in silent endurance but in the courage to speak difficult truths. My journey with Nick taught me that love without honesty is merely comfort disguised as devotion—a beautiful façade masking a crumbling foundation.

The years I spent swallowing my words, believing I was practicing self-control, only enabled the very destruction I feared confronting. When I finally found my voice that night in the hospital, I discovered that truth—even painful truth—creates space for genuine healing to begin.

For anyone walking alongside a loved one battling addiction, know that your silence, however well-intentioned, may become the very chains that bind both of you. Love demands more than quiet suffering; it requires the bravery to speak when remaining silent would be the easier path.

The greatest gift I received from my broken relationship wasn't the brief moments of happiness but the profound understanding that boundaries aren't rejection—they're love at its most mature. I learned that carrying someone's **secret** isn't the same as carrying their ***burden***, and that sometimes, letting go is the most loving act possible.

If you find yourself trapped in the exhausting cycle of loving someone through addiction, please don't walk this path alone. Reach out, share your story, and allow others to help shoulder your pain. Remember that honesty, both with yourself and your loved one, isn't cruelty—it's the foundation upon which genuine healing can begin.

In the end, loving Nick taught me that true compassion values long-term wholeness over temporary peace, and that sometimes, love speaks loudest when it breaks the silence. That, my friend, is self-control in action.

Keywana Wright-Jones

Dedication: I dedicate this to my daughter, Tayler. I pray she practices self-control as she grows in faith and into adulthood. My heart's desire is that the Holy Spirit guides her, helping her resist temptations and make the best decisions in life.

Bio: Keywana Wright-Jones is a native of Flint, Michigan, where she resides with her husband and daughter. She is a five-time Amazon Bestselling Author and serves as an Associate Pastor at her church. She enjoys writing short devotions and teaching the Word of God during Sunday school. Keywana has 19 years of experience in human services and works at the Michigan Department of Human Services.

A Believer's Life Necessitates Self-Control

"He that hath no rule over his own spirit is like a city that is broken down and without a wall." (Proverbs 25:28).

Have you ever experienced a time when you found it difficult to exercise self-control? According to an online dictionary, "Self-control is the ability to manage your impulses, emotions, and behaviors when facing immediate temptations or distractions."

As a child, I struggled to resist my craving for sweets, especially before dinner. I tried many times to resist my temptations for treats, but my weakness for chocolate chip cookies and vanilla ice cream often got the best of me. I remember getting in trouble for sneaking ice cream one day before dinner. Even as children, we start to learn about self-control and the consequences of not practicing it. One of the toughest challenges for people is being patient and managing their desires.

God knew self-control would be difficult for mankind, as we see in Genesis with Adam and Eve and how they disobeyed by eating from the forbidden tree. It was Eve's curiosity that led her to the forbidden fruit. She had a moment of struggle with self-control, which ultimately overcame her. She wondered in her mind, "Would we surely die if we ate from that tree?" The serpent told her, "You don't die." She believed the serpent and ate. That day, sin entered the world.

When one lacks self-control in their life, it can lead to chaos. Having self-control is essential, and practicing it is crucial for the believer. It's a gift from God and should be evident in every believer's life. Self-control is a discipline given by the Holy Spirit that enables Christians to resist the power of the flesh. According to Galatians 5:25, if we live by the Spirit, let us also keep in step with the Spirit. The Holy Spirit dwells within the believer and helps to put self-control into practice.

However, in contrast, someone who exercises self-control rules over their flesh. As Apostle Paul instructs in Galatians 5:24, we must deny our flesh. "Those in Christ have crucified the flesh with its passions and desires." When we walk according to the Spirit, we deny our worldly ways. Our desires align with God's desires for us.

Here are a few benefits of promoting self-control in your life:

- Being able to resist temptations.
- Managing your emotions and behaviors.
- Meeting personal and professional goals.
- Making sound decisions.

In conclusion, as you practice self-control in your life, you will be able to live free from errors and sins. Remember this: it's a daily task, and it's okay if you don't always meet the mark. Just know you can try again tomorrow. According to Proverbs 16:32, *"He that is slow to anger is better than the mighty, and he that ruleth his spirit than he that taketh a city."*

Let us pray:

Heavenly Father God, I ask that You bless those who read this with self-control. Help them to exercise self-control daily and resist temptation. I pray they will walk according to the Spirit rather than their flesh. In Jesus' name, Amen.

Reyna Harris-Goynes

Dedication: My story is dedicated to other women who may be facing similar birthing situations as I did in the past. To you, I say: Keep going, ladies! You got this!

Bio: Reyna Harris-Goynes is the wife of an awesome and loving husband, a mother of five, and a grandmother of three. She owns two businesses: V.R. Fashions & More, and V.R. Mobile Notary. Reyna and her family are residents of the Houston, Texas area.

A Mother to "All of Them"

Many people don't know the depths of my life story. I can now share that I've gone through some tough and very challenging times. But nothing has been harder than losing a child I never got to meet outside the womb. I've had miscarriages and two abortions, the latter of which was never by choice.

Dealing with a miscarriage presents its own challenges, but processing the aftermath makes it even harder to move past the loss. Additionally, the people who are supposed to be in your corner—whether good or bad—sometimes turn their backs on you. It was tough to handle, which forced me to become a stronger person over the years. I have only a few people in my support system because it's hard to talk about these things with others without feeling judged.

There was a time when I struggled with depression and felt ashamed about experiencing miscarriages and abortions. I felt isolated and believed that no one cared or showed sympathy for me and my "situations." In fact, the only advice I ever received each time was, "That's a part of life, Reyna. Move on."

In 2018, while coping with my son's battle with cancer, I received the news that I was pregnant again. After a healthy pregnancy, I believed everything would go smoothly and I could carry the baby to term. Suddenly, I started experiencing stomach pains. I went to the emergency room, and they told me they didn't see anything wrong, so they sent me home and advised me to see my OB/GYN. The pains lessened somewhat between visits, but they never fully went away. During my OB/GYN appointment, they delivered some devastating news:

"We don't see a baby or hear a heartbeat."

That news crushed me, but I moved on. In 2019, I became pregnant again. Around the same time, my son's doctor told my husband and me that the cancer was back... again. The stress from that diagnosis overwhelmed me, and I lost that baby, too.

I fell into a deep darkness after my miscarriage in 2019 that I thought I'd never recover from. I believed the child would be a turning point in my marriage and that the baby was what our little family needed during that difficult time, considering everything we were going through. On top of everything, I was also dealing with all my husband's legal issues.

I remember the day God told me, "It's not going to happen the way you think." As a believer in Him and His Word, I know He has His own way of working things out in His time. At this point, I believe we don't need another child—although I often wonder, "What if all my babies lived?"

BUT GOD! You got this, Reyna!

1996. 1999. 2000. 2018. 2019. Gone... But Never Forgotten.

****

Editor's Note: Finding Strength After Trauma

Dear Readers,

In the rawness of Reyna's story, many of you might see reflections of your own journey—the unspoken grief of pregnancy loss, the burden of tough medical choices, or the overwhelming loneliness that comes with trauma. If her words touched you, even just a little, please remember this: you are not alone, and your story is important.

As I reflect on Reyna's experiences and the many similar stories I've heard over the years, I am reminded of the wisdom in Galatians 5:23, which talks about self-control as a Fruit of the Spirit. That trait—often misunderstood as just restraint—is actually a deep source of healing for those navigating the aftereffects of trauma.

Self-control, in the context of healing, isn't about suppressing emotions or "getting over" your loss. Instead, it's about creating space between your trauma responses and your actions—allowing yourself to feel deeply while choosing how you move forward. It's permission to grieve while refusing to let grief define your entire existence.

I remember talking with a woman who had gone through her fourth miscarriage. "I feel like my body is betraying me," she whispered, "and my thoughts are even worse. They're telling me I don't deserve to be a mother." In that moment, she was practicing self-control—not by denying her thoughts, but by recognizing them without surrendering to them. Months later, she told me how that distinction had changed everything: "I still have those thoughts sometimes, but they no longer own me."

For those walking similar paths, here are some gentle practices that might help cultivate self-control in your healing journey:

- **Set boundaries around your story.** Decide who should hear your vulnerability and who shouldn't. As

Reyna mentioned, sometimes even those who are supposed to support us can't or won't. Self-control involves protecting your narrative from those who might diminish it.

- **Create mindfulness rituals.** When overwhelming emotions surface, ground yourself through breath work or sensory awareness exercises. That creates the vital pause between feeling and reaction, allowing for deliberate choices rather than impulsive responses.
- **Practice compassionate self-talk.** Notice when your inner dialogue becomes accusatory—"I should have..." or "If only I had..."—and gently redirect it. Self-control includes refusing to be cruel to yourself about circumstances beyond your control.
- **Connect with a community of people who understand.** Sharing with others who have walked similar paths can provide validation without judgment, offering a sense of camaraderie and understanding. Those connections will remind you that your experiences, while uniquely yours, are not isolated phenomena.

The road of healing is neither straight nor short. Some days, self-control might look like simply getting out of bed and planting your feet on the floor. Other days, it might mean allowing yourself to cry when memories resurface unexpectedly. Throughout it all, remember that this Fruit of the Spirit develops slowly, often during seasons when we feel the furthest from God's comfort.

Like Reyna, who found the strength to declare "BUT GOD! You got this, Reyna!" in her darkest moments, I pray you discover the profound power of choosing your response to circumstances you never chose. Your losses are not forgotten—

not by those who love you, not by the divine presence that holds you, and certainly not by the community of fellow "travelers" who understand the terrain of that arduous journey.

With love, hope, and solidarity,
Angela Edwards, Editor

Precious Damas

Dedication: To my Heavenly Father: Thank You for Your unending grace and mercy. To my family—my husband, children, grandchildren, and loved ones: Your love is my steady place. To every reader who finds these pages in a time of need: May you feel the quiet power of the pause.

Bio: Precious Damas is a woman of faith, a devoted wife, mother, and grandmother, and a trusted friend to many. As the author of the Mask Off book series and four bestselling Christian titles she contributed to, she writes to encourage the weary, uplift those searching, and glorify God in every word. Her latest contribution to God's Self-Control Fruit invites readers on a collective journey with 15 unique voices. Precious' prayer is simple: May her words meet you in your moment and point you toward the grace of God that never runs out.

The Power of the Pause

Self-control is strength. Calmness is mastery. You must get to a point where your mood doesn't change based on the significant actions of others. Don't let anyone control your life.

The Power of the Pause – 12.01.1989

I knew I had activated my self-control the day my mother and I almost got into a physical fist fight. At the time, I was fed up. The only thing on my mind was getting my little brother to the hospital.

I remember the moment well...

I came home from school, hungrier than a stray dog roaming the neighborhood with mange. Like any other day, I entered an apartment I once called home. I went straight to my bedroom, which I used to call my "safe space," but that wasn't the case anymore. Ever since my sister moved in with my aunt (because she was out of control), I was left alone to fend for myself. I had vowed not to leave my mother alone in the apartment with the drug addicts and their lifestyle. I mean, she was my mother, and I was her firstborn. How could I just leave her? As I entered my safe space, I immediately noticed people sleeping on my sister's bunk beds—one at the bottom, and another at the top (there were two sets of bunk beds in the room; no one was sleeping on mine). I stood in the doorway of the room, one foot in and one foot out, not knowing what to think. I dared not ask because I knew I would've lost control.

My mom came up from behind me and said, "They're just sleeping. Here is $20.00. Why don't you go and get yourself something to eat?" As I gazed into her dilated pupils, she slowly

30

turned away from me, avoiding eye contact. Still, I knew what was happening—her slow ability to communicate, her anxious desire to return to the kitchen and the people there. I knew... *I knew.*

I gently took the money out of her hand, even though I wanted to snatch it and push her into the wall. I couldn't do it, though, because she's my mother—and I still needed her. I watched as her petite 5'2" pregnant frame walked away, leaving me standing there. I left the apartment and went to my other safe space, which was my aunt's house, knowing I'd be able to get a meal and be around people who loved me.

When I arrived, I went straight to my sister. I missed her so much and needed to be close. I was happiest when we were together. We were like two peas in a pod. I avoided my aunt as long as I could because I knew she would ask me how my mother was doing. When that moment came, I replied, "She's good." My aunt knew I was lying through my teeth.

The moment I left my aunt's house, sadness and anger immediately returned. I had to regain my composure before walking back into my home. I can't remember if I asked God for help. Honestly, I don't recall ever asking Him for help when I was young. What I do remember clearly is often feeling utterly alone in this world.

Self-Control – 1.17.1990

It was Monday morning, and I was looking forward to going to my other safe space: school. I felt safe there because I had a few teachers I trusted who knew my story. At the same time, I felt like I kept telling the same story over and over again but wasn't getting any help. I was around friends who were going through the exact same things, so they understood. I was always a loner because I often wanted to explode on anyone and everyone in the blink of an eye.

After school, as I approached my building, I was told my mother had been taken to the hospital in an ambulance. My first thought was that she got hurt by one of the dealers or overdosed. Then I thought, "It's the baby!" I quickly went to my aunt's house, where I was told my mother had the baby. My aunt was on her way there, so I jumped in the car with her.

As we approached my mother's room, we encountered her doctor at the door. He asked if we were family members, and we replied yes. We followed the doctor inside, where he told my mother that drugs were found in the baby's system. She turned her head and looked at the wall. The doctor left, and my aunt went to talk with him. When she came back, I noticed her whole demeanor had changed.

The ride home that day was eerily quiet. When my aunt finally spoke, she said they had, indeed, found drugs in the baby's system and that she wasn't sure what would happen to the baby for a couple of days. I remember going home to grab some clothes because I refused to stay in that unsafe place alone.

The hospital discharged my mother and the baby, with a nurse agreeing to visit weekly to monitor the baby's health and progress. That routine lasted for about a month before the addicts returned, and my parents once again became consumed by their drugs and "friends."

There was a big difference between before and after, as I now had to look out not only for myself but also for my little brother. As a big sister, I did my best to protect my little brother by making sure he was fed, had his diaper changed, and wore clean pajamas. At one point, I found myself losing self-control when I noticed he had a breathing problem. He had been home for only two months at the time.

I remember coming home one day to an apartment full of people, and it was smoky. Before even setting my bookbag down, I went to check on my brother. I heard him crying loudly, not understanding why my mother didn't tend to his needs. When I reached him, what I saw was unusual. As I leaned over the crib and looked into my baby brother's eyes, it seemed like blood was about to pour out of his tear ducts. That scared me terribly. I called my aunt to let her know, and she told me to get him dressed and meet her downstairs. As I dressed him, I noticed his skin was hard and scaly, like a turtle's shell. I jumped back in fear, knowing something was desperately wrong.

My mother came in a short time later, asking what I was doing. I told her my brother wasn't breathing well and that I was taking him to the hospital. She replied, "The hospital? He already has an appointment scheduled for March 29th."

"March 29th?" I yelled. "It's February 17th. He's not going to make it to the end of March!" I felt myself losing my self-control at that moment. "I'm taking him, and Auntie is coming to get us!"

She snatched the baby bag from me, and that was the last button I let her press. When she grabbed the bag, she also pushed me to the ground. As much as I wanted to unleash the wrath of God on her, I didn't. I didn't know much about the Bible, but I knew there was a commandment about honoring mothers and fathers. I just got up, grabbed my baby brother, and headed downstairs—all while praying she wouldn't follow me. She didn't.

We Were Going to a Safe Place

When we arrived at the hospital, they quickly took my brother away for an examination. It took quite a while. After about an hour or so, a social worker came to see us. She asked me where my mother was, and before I could think about the best response, I blurted out, "She's at home, doing crack."

"Well, I need to let you both know that the baby will not be going back to her. There is cocaine in his system," she replied.

Talk about being stunned into silence! My aunt and I looked at each other, wondering which one of us would share the news with my mother. Suddenly, we heard a familiar voice ask, "Where is my baby?" It was my mother. She called the police to give her a ride! Can you believe that?

About ten minutes later, my mother's older sister arrived. My aunt and I exchanged glances, both apparently thinking the same thing: "That's who's going to tell her!" While my mother was with the baby, my aunt informed her sister about what the social worker said. Since my older aunt was a foster parent, we were confident my brother would go to her home.

A short while later, the doctors and social worker came out with my mother to update us. Baby J was doing well, and his oxygen levels were gradually returning to normal. They also said they would give him oatmeal baths around the clock to soothe his eczema.

The doctor looked at me and said, "You saved your brother's life. If he had spent another night in that environment, he may not have made it."

I felt that. I truly did.

Custody Battle

At home, I walked on eggshells, fearful of what my mother might do to me in response to saving my brother's life, but every time I thought about what the doctor said to me, I feared what I might do to her! I'm grateful for the gentle voice inside of me that told me to calm down, focus on myself, and do what was necessary to get out of there. I hate to admit it, but I didn't feel safe whatsoever in my own home.

I continued to attend school and spend more and more time at my aunt's house with my sister. I recall when my aunt informed me that my brother would be coming home from the hospital in a week. I was so happy to hear that, I almost cried. I asked her if she thought it would be a good idea to move in with my other aunt so I could be closer to my brother. She replied, "I think that would be the best thing for both of you."

The Conclusion

At a young age, I had to learn how to tap into my self-control. I gained so many headaches during that time that it made me so angry inside. Over time, I grew to understand the importance of self-control, especially when I began to study

Bible stories. Several individuals in the Bible who demonstrated self-control include Jesus, David, Daniel, and Abigail.

- Jesus was unsuccessfully tempted by Satan during his 40 days and nights in the wilderness after His baptism.
- David spared King Saul's life instead of killing him.
- Daniel refused to defile his body with the king's food and wine.
- Abigail's quick thinking prevented David and his men from carrying out a massacre.

As for me, I showed self-control by being obedient and not disrespecting my mother.

I conclude my story by saying this: Self-control is already within you. Discipline, willpower, and a genuine understanding of oneself and others will take you far and give you peace and power over your own life.

"Honor your father and mother—which is the first commandment with a promise—so that it may go well with you and that you may enjoy long life on the earth" (Ephesians 6:2-3, NIV).

Tosha R. Dearbone

Dedication: To every soul who has ever gone to the wrong well, may you know the Living Water that restores, renews, and teaches you the power of self-control. Your past is not your prison; it's the platform that God will use to pour life into others.

Bio: Tosha Dearbone was born in Urania, Louisiana, and raised in Missouri City, Texas. She is a mother of four, grandmother of three, and a significant presence in her community as a youth advocate. Tosha specializes in the medical field at Texas Children's Hospital, where she has developed skills and received training to work with adolescents daily over the past 18 years. She is the founder of Positive Express, a nonprofit organization, mentors youths in the juvenile system, and serves as the Youth Director at Transforming Faith Christian Center. Connect with Tosha on social media at Tosha R Dearbone or email at trdearbo@yahoo.com.

My Fruit Matters

For many years, the Holy Spirit whispered to me about the woman at the well (as found in John 4:1-42), but I didn't realize why it was significant until recently. You see, the story about the woman wasn't just about being seen by Jesus; it was about how one moment of truth and love redirected her life. She had a past full of broken relationships and was likely emotionally and spiritually unstable. But what really changed her was meeting Jesus, who revealed her truth and offered her a better way to "transform."

After she met Jesus, she left her jar behind—symbolizing a departure from her old patterns. She went back to her hometown, where shame once dwelled, and chose to testify instead of hide. That requires emotional maturity, spiritual discipline, and a surrendered will, all grounded in self-control through the power of the Spirit.

Now, let's look at what I like to call my "Mystery Story."

For me to transform, I had to do some work myself. I compare part of my story to that of the woman at the well. The community shamed her because she had been married five times, only for Jesus to tell her that the man she was with at the time wasn't even her husband. I like to believe that her marriages were her way of seeking fulfillment, similar to how I moved from relationship to relationship with different men, trying to fill a void—a void that was deeper than just wanting to be with a man. I struggled because I didn't know my identity. I didn't feel like I fit in because I didn't understand the longing that kept driving me as I searched for answers to my questions. I wanted—***needed***—to know more about where I came from.

Eventually, I reached a point where I believed I couldn't go back to those broken sources, searching for love, peace, and purpose, because each time, I was left feeling empty. I didn't realize that what I truly needed wasn't another relationship, escape, or certification. I needed Living Water—something that would fulfill me from within.

Maybe now you understand why the woman at the well visited in the middle of the day. Jesus met her in the midst of her "mess," not after she had cleaned up. You see, Jesus didn't shame the woman. He revealed the truth and offered her more than she could ever imagine. But like the saying goes, "If He can do it for her, He can do it for me," so He did.

That was when I turned the mirror around and did my own self-evaluation. Did God come and clean me up amid my mess? He absolutely did! I had yet to start thinking about therapy or even recognize that I needed to heal before my transformation began.

But let me back up just a little...

By the age of 25, I had endured abuse from men, their families, and even my own family. In each case, I wanted to believe they loved me. Instead, I was rejected, cheated on, and impregnated, only to be left to figure life out on my own. Eventually, I grew tired of the chaos. I no longer wanted to stay trapped in that repetitive cycle and longed for better for my children and myself. So, I asked God to remove my desire to be in a relationship and to hide me.

Now, let me say this: When I asked God to do those things, I didn't honestly believe He would do what I asked, but

He did. He even removed their families from my life as well. Praise God!

In the aftermath, it felt as though I had become invisible to men, with Jesus being the only one who could now see and hear me. I would wake up at 5:00 a.m. every day, pray, have coffee, and then ask God to guide my day, with the understanding that whatever happened during the day was already pre-ordained.

Regarding my family, I struggled a bit longer because I wanted their acceptance. I yearned for them to see me and hear my every thought. Instead, they shunned me for getting pregnant at a young age and said things no daughter or sibling should hear from her own family. In response, I isolated myself and moved away at 16 years old. Among the reasons for that decision was to prove I could be independent and care for my child on my own, and to avoid being a burden to anyone. During that time, I stayed focused and grew even more committed to seeking Jesus. He became my everything. I was so focused on Him that I didn't even realize I was walking in self-control while healing at the same time. That journey became part of my strength and daily focus.

I no longer operated from a broken cycle of those who didn't accept, love, or care about me. Instead, I prospered by setting boundaries, breaking soul ties, changing my mindset, and protecting my peace.

"So, above all, guard the affections of your heart, for they affect all that you are. Pay attention to the welfare of your innermost being, for from there flows the wellspring of life" (Proverbs 4:23, TPT).

The water from that wellspring came with a price, though. I had to choose it every day. I had to learn how to say no to things that drained me. I had to develop self-control, not out of fear but because I finally knew I was worthy. My life's mystery was never about being lost; it was about being found. And now, like the woman at the well, I speak up so that others can find their way, too!

Considering everything I had experienced, I believe if the enemy had been able to keep me emotionally craving love and acceptance, he would have prevented me from responding spiritually. For others to receive spiritual guidance, I could not be unstable in my ways.

"The heart is deceitful above all things and beyond cure. Who can understand it?" (Jeremiah 17:9).

Fast forward to today. I am 45 years old, living out loud, and doing what God has called me to do. I own and operate a nonprofit organization called Positive Express, where I get to empower girls through mentorship rooted in faith, self-worth, and resilience. Now in our 12th year, I am proud to say that even through ups and downs, we are still going strong. My experience of being obedient to this calling has taught me that, just as it was for the girls, it was also for me to heal. I had to face my past traumatic experiences head-on. The turning point in my journey came when truth collided with chaos, and I was offered something better.

I am also a facilitator at a men's prison in Richmond, Texas, through an organization called Bridges to Life, where I have the opportunity to support inmates on their journey of restoration. Additionally, I oversee the youth program at my church (ages three to ten), which helps me grow closer to God through studies aimed at training the next generation of believers in Christ Jesus.

So, when you feel like you can't gain self-control in your life, I say, "If I can do it, you can do it, too!" It's all about your mindset.

"For as a man thinketh in his heart, so is he" (Proverbs 23:7).

Don't waver to the left or right for too long. Know that if you are walking with God, *"...you can do all things through Christ who strengthens you"* (Philippians 4:13).

I ask you: What Fruit of the Spirit do you see active in your life right now? Is it helping you stay connected to God, life, and your purpose? If so, then you are already on the right path! Is self-control something you have or want to develop to reach the next level? To do so, you need a changed and focused mindset.

As I conclude my story, I would like to share something else that demonstrates the results of my self-control. I'm currently in school, working two jobs, running a nonprofit, and managing life with an incarcerated son. Will I say it's been easy? Not at all. Instead, it has been challenging, to say the least, but having self-control to guide and protect me has helped me stay focused and determined as I work toward every goal that has been set.

As my pastor would say, "Finish the race, complete the work, and get the job done!"

Self-control is your portion. Receive it and use it wisely, not allowing distractions to overtake what God has already put in place. I pray my story gives you freedom to know you are more than what you've been through.

Dr. Joanne B. Lewis

Dedication: To my family, ancestors, and my angels—my mother, Armielee Hughley Ballard, my sweet sister-in-luv, my Tina, and my other Tina: I will forever feel the love from all of you. I am full of dreams that are coming to fruition. I thank You, Lord. I know I. AM. Enough.

Bio: Dr. Joanne B. Lewis is a servant of God, a retired Ohio-licensed social worker and educator, a seven-time bestselling author, and a magazine contributor. She advocates for people living their best lives and is the Founder, CEO, and Owner of Hope for Today, LLC, a nonprofit organization dedicated to spreading positive awareness and inspiration. Dr. Lewis is a member of Alpha Kappa Alpha Sorority, Inc., and a dedicated, compassionate, and courageous keynote speaker. For more information about her upcoming book, to discuss booking her for your next event, or to purchase books, visit her website at iamjoanneblewis1.com or email jblewish1908@yahoo.com.

Healing from Within

"But the fruit of the Spirit is love, joy, peace, forbearance, kindness, goodness, faithfulness, gentleness, and self-control. Against such things, there is no law" (Galatians 5:22-23, NIV).

I had never paid much attention to the last fruit listed in the scripture above—self-control. As an adult, I have experienced emotional abuse, verbal abuse, and been ghosted. Ghosting occurs when someone abruptly stops all communication without providing an explanation. All those actions against me greatly impacted my self-esteem and deeply hurt my feelings. I had yet to learn how to guard my heart and feelings, as instructed in Proverbs 4:23 (NIV):

"Above all else, guard your heart, for everything you do flows from it."

I grew up not realizing I was solely responsible for my mental and emotional health. Although I didn't know it, I was tasked with setting and maintaining safe boundaries to protect myself. There was no knight in shining armor to save me, no prince on a horse to rescue me from danger. I was already saved and protected by God's love and grace. When God created me, He gave me strength that would sustain me throughout my life.

However, amid my "stinkin-thinkin," I had decided that I was not "good enough" and shouldn't expect to be treated differently. Still, I couldn't understand why mental and emotional abuse kept affecting my life. I had to figure out what I did or said that caused someone to disappear from my life, to stop all communication with me. What had I done or said that made them say hurtful things? After all, I thought we were good.

45

There had been no disagreements or anything like that. I remembered birthdays and checked in to offer support and encouragement—things I did regularly for my family, both biological and chosen. I was a stand-up hype woman for everyone but myself.

I was living in a space of fear—fear of this and that, afraid of abandonment, and more. Living in that space was paralyzing.

"For the Spirit God gave us does not make us timid, but gives us power, love, and self-discipline" (1 Timothy 1:7, NIV).

I refused to depend on God, though. I wanted friends who would treat me with kindness the same way I treated others. However, God was showing me that I needed to depend ONLY on Him. I had the ability to practice self-control, but I lacked the will to submit to God. I described myself as a people-pleaser and an intuitive empath.

A brief definition of a "people-pleaser" is someone who tries to make others happy even if it conflicts with their own feelings. That person might fear being abandoned and tend to avoid conflict.

A brief definition of an "intuitive empath" is someone who is highly sensitive to others' emotions and can understand and empathize with their feelings.

I was the lone instructor in teaching people that it was okay to ignore my feelings, be disrespectful to me, or speak harshly to me. I showed them that I was stuck in people-pleasing mode, afraid to end any relationship, even if it wasn't good for me. I taught them that I would keep giving until I had nothing left to offer, then apologize for not having more to give.

Those same people started to expect a quick apology from me whenever I felt any discomfort in the relationship, just to get things back on track. I also taught them how easily I would manipulate myself to remain in a dysfunctional relationship, and that I would listen to their problems and offer my professional opinion and resources.

I seemingly welcomed dysfunction by constructing a revolving door in my heart, allowing them to enter my life, berate me, leave, and return later to start over again as if nothing had ever happened.

The "lessons" I taught guided people to aim for the 'X' on my heart that marked the spot. I was a good instructor and truly taught them well. They knew I would never defend myself in conflict because reacting was uncomfortable for me. My experience growing up was that when I was the target of a verbally abusive rant, it was better to stay silent for fear of a physical attack. Being in defensive mode was unfamiliar territory for me. I usually tried to remain outwardly calm and maintain a steady tone of voice, focusing on not succumbing to the fear of the moment. I knew I deserved better, and I believed it.

I will never forget the moment I knew I was in the presence of God. The time finally came when I realized I was about to start living in the power that God granted me, including practicing self-control. I began to feel a gentle healing wash over me—an awakening of my entire being in my faith. I had made my free-will decision to live according to each Fruit of the Spirit. I knew I was blessed by God's love for me. I learned the lesson and chose to live in God's Fruit every day.

I have been forever changed by the **love** Christ has for me. I experience immeasurable **joy** and contentment in my relationship with God. **Peace** fills my soul. I understand the gift of patience and the power of choosing **forbearance**. I smile when showing **kindness** and selfless **goodness**, trusting in God's **faithfulness** to His word, and practicing **gentleness** by being patient with others. **SELF-CONTROL** is the intentional act of living my life as Christ has ordained.

I am forever grateful for my life, knowing that my testimony will one day help someone who is struggling, whether in relationships with parents, children, at work, at church, or anywhere else. My beloved mother would tell us, "You want to find yourself doing the right thing in whatever you do when Jesus comes."

Katina Rice-Davis

Dedication: I dedicate this chapter to every soul learning the beauty of restraint, not as weakness but as strength. May these words remind you that true self-control is birthed by the Spirit within, guiding us toward peace, wisdom, and victory over impulses that once ruled us.

Bio: Katina Rice-Davis is a seven-time Bestselling Author, Inspirational Speaker, and Human-Interest Journalist with The Woodruff Times. A native of Cross Anchor, South Carolina, she transforms her personal journey of loss and resilience into a source of empowerment for others. After her husband's unexpected passing, Katina turned to writing as a healing outlet, which blossomed into a career of storytelling and advocacy. With grace and grit, Katina inspires others to find purpose after pain and rise with faith, courage, and hope. Contact Katina at ykdavis43@gmail.com.

The Strength Within

When I reflect on my journey from a fiery, impulsive young woman to a seasoned adult walking in step with the Spirit, the virtue that has stood out most distinctly is self-control. Not the kind of restraint born out of pride or fear of consequences, but the kind nurtured and cultivated by the Holy Spirit—gracefully, patiently, and powerfully. The Bible calls it a "Fruit of the Spirit" for good reason. It is not something we manufacture on our own. It blossoms in our lives when we yield ourselves daily to God's will.

Galatians 5:22-23 lists self-control as the final fruit in a beautiful array of spiritual virtues. In my early walk with Christ, I didn't understand its importance. I knew to be kind, to love, and to have faith, but self-control felt like a far-off goal— something reserved for monks or the ultra-disciplined. But life, with its challenges, relationships, and temptations, taught me otherwise. I learned that without self-control, love can become suffocating, joy can turn into diligence, and zeal can slip into arrogance.

In my youth, I responded to offenses with swift words and even swifter judgments. I was quick-tempered and proud, often believing that reacting immediately somehow made me strong. People who tried to push my buttons found an easy target. I didn't pause to pray or consider that my response was more about my character than their provocation. But the Holy Spirit has a gentle way of nudging us toward truth, and in time, I began to see the damage my lack of self-control caused—to others and to my own soul.

Growth didn't happen overnight, though. It came through prayer, humility, and failing forward. I remember moments when someone insulted or misjudged me, and my old self itched to lash out. That was when the Spirit whispered, "Hold your tongue." At first, silence felt like defeat, but over time, I realized that true strength lies not in dominating a conversation but in mastering myself. Now, when people try to provoke me, I don't react the way they expect. Instead, I respond calmly, sometimes with silence but always with intention. That isn't weakness; it's wisdom and spiritual maturity that teaches those around me, especially my children and grandson, that there is a better way to live.

I used to be guided by my emotions. I followed wherever anger, fear, anxiety, and even happiness led me. But emotions are fleeting and fickle. They can deceive us and steer us away from God's best. I've learned to seek guidance from the Spirit instead. The world says, "Follow your heart," but Jeremiah 17:9 (NIV) warns us: *"The heart is deceitful above all things and beyond cure..."*

Notably, there's a difference between reacting and responding. Reacting is often impulsive, emotional, and self-centered. Responding requires thought, prayer, and perspective. When I think before I speak, I make room for the Spirit to guide my words. Proverbs 15:1 (NIV) says, *"A gentle answer turns away wrath, but a harsh word stirs up anger."* Choosing gentleness and wisdom over rage has changed the atmosphere in my home and within myself.

Self-control isn't about suppression but submission to God. It means choosing His way, even when everything inside you screams for a different path. It's the restraint that keeps us from gossiping, the patience that preserves our peace, and the discipline that resists temptation. As a mother and now a grandmother, I am keenly aware that I am being watched. My actions preach louder than any words ever could. My prayer is that my life becomes a model of discipline—Spirit-led living, not perfection but pursuit. I want my children and grandson to see that it is possible to say no to the flesh and yes to God.

Self-control spills into every aspect of life, from how we handle money to how we treat others, care for our bodies, and respond to adversity. It is not compartmentalized; it is comprehensive. The Apostle Paul wrote in 1 Corinthians 9:25-27 about disciplining his body and keeping it under control like an athlete preparing for a race. That metaphor resonates with me deeply. Every choice we make trains us for righteousness... or not. Every small victory matters.

Even amid grief, disappointment, and loss, I have found that self-control keeps me grounded in God's peace. When emotions threaten to overwhelm me and loneliness creeps in, I remind myself that indulging in despair or bitterness won't lead to healing. Self-control helps me realign with God's truth when feelings try to hijack my faith.

Titus 2:11-12 tells us that God's grace teaches us to say "no" to ungodliness and worldly passions, and to live self-controlled, upright, and godly lives in this present age. The word "teach" implies a process. We don't wake up one day immune to temptation. We are taught by grace, and grace is patient. Each time we deny our sinful nature, we strengthen our spirit. I've said no to relationships that weren't God-honoring, to conversations that could've led to division, and to behaviors that once seemed harmless but now clearly dishonor God. I've said no to overindulging, to retaliation, and to self-pity. Conversely, I've said yes to peace, forgiveness, self-respect, and obedience.

Self-control often remains unseen by the world, but it is always visible to God. He observes your decision to walk away, to bite your tongue, and to close your mouth in prayer instead of lashing out. He sees you choosing virtue over vice, grace over gossip, and worship over worry. Many don't realize that self-control is a form of spiritual warfare. It involves taking our thoughts captive and resisting the devil so that he flees. It's not just about willpower but about divine empowerment. The Holy Spirit within us strengthens us to overcome.

There's freedom in restraint. That may sound ironic, but it's true. When the Spirit leads us, we are no longer slaves to sin. We walk in true liberty—the freedom to live as God designed us to live. The world calls restraint "restrictive," but God calls it "righteous." Romans 12:2 (NIV) says, *"Do not conform to the pattern of this world, but be transformed by the renewing of your mind."* That renewal involves restraining our desires, realigning our hearts with Heaven, and resisting the lies of the culture that tell us to chase every whim.

Living a disciplined, righteous life in alignment with God's will doesn't mean I never fall short. But now, I fall forward into grace, growth, and God's arms. Self-control has become evidence of my transformation. It's the quiet confidence I carry when storms rage around me. It's the inner strength that speaks louder than anger ever could.

I want to leave behind more than material wealth; I aim to leave a legacy of character. I want my grandchildren to remember not just my love, but my wisdom. Not just my laughter, but my restraint. Not just my presence, but the Spirit within me.

If I could go back and talk to my younger self, I'd say, "Let the Spirit guide you. Don't follow every emotion. Don't give in to every temptation. Choose what pleases God, and you'll find peace that surpasses all understanding."

Let us all remember: Self-control isn't about being perfect. It's about being Spirit-filled. When we allow the Spirit to guide our hearts, what flows out of us reflects the glory of the One who lives within us.

So, today and every day, I choose once again to walk in step with the Spirit and let self-control shape my speech, choices, and legacy. For in that choice lies strength, and in that strength, a life truly flourishing in God's grace.

And when the day comes that my journey here is complete, I pray that others will say of me, not that I never stumbled, not that I was flawless, but that I lived a Spirit-led life marked by discipline, wisdom, and grace. I pray they say I used my strength not to control others, but to control myself. That my life testified to the truth that when we fully surrender to God, He equips us with everything we need to endure, overcome, and flourish.

Prayer for Strength and Self-Control

Heavenly Father,

I come before You with a heart full of gratitude for the lessons You've taught me through the gift of self-control. Thank You for never giving up on me, even when I gave in to my flesh or allowed emotions to lead me astray. Lord, I confess that I cannot walk in true strength apart from Your Spirit. Help me to remember daily that self-control is not my own doing but Your fruit blossoming within me.

Father, train my heart to pause before speaking, to listen before judging, and to love before reacting. Teach me to master my emotions so they will not master me. In moments of temptation, remind me that Your grace is sufficient. When anger rises, let peace be my portion. When fear whispers, let faith answer louder.

Lord, may my life reflect Your discipline and wisdom so that my children, grandchildren, and all who witness my journey will see the beauty of a Spirit-led life. Strengthen me to say "no" to what pulls me from You and "yes" to all that draws me closer. Let my legacy be one of self-control, grace, and unwavering faith.

In Jesus' name, Amen.

Simone Holyfield

Dedication: This heartfelt dedication is to my first love, Jesus Christ, and my three cherished children: Gabriel, Noah, and Naja. Without Christ, my life would lack direction and purpose. He has gifted me the joy of motherhood. Remember to be your own sunshine each day, reflecting on Psalm 46:10: "Be still, and know that I am God."

Bio: Simone Holyfield, also known as Simone Iman, is an inspiring mother of three and a multi-talented, award-winning artist, singer, songwriter, producer, poet, and radio personality. She became a trailblazer as the first African-American artist to sign with Partridge Records, earning her the title "First Lady of Partridge Records." Her debut album, *Kismet*, released in 2009, marked the launch of her influential music career. Beyond her artistic achievements, Simone serves as the DEI Officer in Everett, Massachusetts, where she advocates for diversity and inclusion. Through the "Everett for Everyone" initiative, she empowers her community with cultural programs and celebrations that unite and uplift residents.

Through the Shadows to the Light

My Journey of Heartbreak, Healing, and the Fruit of the Spirit of Self-Control

I once believed I understood love. At 16, that belief was sparked by a faint flutter of a first crush—a moment that made my heart race and filled me with the promise of endless possibilities. I clung to that fleeting feeling, convinced it was the embodiment of everything I craved. I thought I knew what love was, but I was only beginning to learn how deeply hurt and broken the loss of it could leave someone.

At 18, life's lessons came too quickly. I became a mother to a beautiful, fragile being who relied entirely on me. I saw love in my child's innocent eyes and felt the warmth of his tiny hand gripping mine. But even that unconditional love couldn't erase the cruel messages I had absorbed from the world. Rejection and abandonment lurked in every corner of my life, whispering that I was unworthy. I did everything I could to fill the void, clinging to every semblance of affection that promised to validate my existence, even this small child.

I wanted to be loved unconditionally so badly that I let myself believe that certain relationships, filled with promises of forever, represented that love. I remember the man who embraced me—someone who stepped in when I was a broken girl, struggling under the weight of a three-month-old baby. In a moment I thought would define my escape from loneliness, I married him, convinced that love had finally come to rescue me from all the hurt and pain. I even prayed that our family, soon to be complete with another son, would bring lasting stability and joy.

57

But each time I thought I had found love, the truth shattered me anew. The perfect picture I had painted was nothing more than a mirage and a mask—lingering lies wrapped in a self-centered dream that was never truly about love but rather about filling an emptiness within me. The deception was profound: I was chasing love as if it were a guarantee, never realizing that I was expecting to receive without ever giving what love truly requires. I had no self-control.

The Descent into Darkness

When so-called love failed, pain moved in like an unwelcome yet inescapable companion. It was predictable, unyielding, and, in some terrible way, familiar. At least pain was honest in its constancy. I started to think that, if I couldn't experience love, I might as well feel something—even if that something was agony.

I found myself in a spiral of self-destruction. In the absence of love, I embraced what hurt me: the destructive pull of alcohol, reckless sexual encounters, and violent men who scarred my body and soul. I felt almost numb as I allowed each new trauma to mask the emptiness inside me. Even as I physically hurt, even as I self-mutilated in desperate attempts to feel something, there was a perverse comfort in the familiarity of the pain. I was out of control.

What I didn't see was that those choices were only deepening my wounds. Every time I turned away from love, I invited another layer of darkness. My life became a vicious cycle: the more pitiable my condition became, the more I allowed the abuse and betrayal of relationships to affirm the lie that I was unworthy of love. I was being taught—day in and day out—that pain was safe, more predictable, and more honest than the unpredictable ghost of unconditional love.

The Darkness Within: A Lifetime of Hurt

I can't lie about the depths to which I descended. I was abused from a very early age. In a world where too many of us are taught that we deserve pain, I internalized that belief. The ones who were supposed to protect me became the very ones to imprint the lessons of hurt on my soul. I was beaten and degraded by those who knew better, reinforced by a system of silence that told me my pain was normal—that it was the natural order of things for "someone like me."

In my home, I absorbed the bitter truth: we were made to suffer, to endure, and to be punished for simply existing. From childhood through my teenage years, physical and emotional abuse were constant companions. Those experiences taught me that love was something that came with conditions— a currency that had to be earned through sacrifice or, worse, fear.

My body and mind bore the marks of that dark past. I was violated, abused, and made to feel that my very essence was tainted beyond repair. Each violation drove home the message of worthlessness, embedding itself in my mind until I believed I deserved nothing better. I learned early that in a world that was so relentlessly cruel, numbness—and pain—were preferable to the raw, gut-wrenching terror of loneliness.

Rock Bottom: When Pain Became the Only Truth

There came a point when it all felt like too much—when the weight of my experiences nearly choked the very air from my lungs. I was living amid ruins, battling daily against a tide of self-hatred and despair. In that darkness, I surrendered to the familiar companion of pain. If love felt too fragile and elusive, at least pain was something I could hold onto. That brokenness led to my divorce and a broken home. It also led to a fractured relationship with God.

I'm not proud of those moments. I know too well the cost of trading hope for agony, and it nearly cost me my life. I was trapped in relationships that deepened my wounds further, each betrayal a nail in the coffin of who I once hoped to be. I allowed violence to become a language I understood too well. I let alcohol and fleeting encounters fill the emptiness, even when every high left me feeling lower than before.

I remember nights when I woke up in the cold silence, my body protesting the decisions made long ago. In those moments, I was overwhelmed by a deep emptiness that no physical pain could truly replicate. I had come to believe that perhaps feeling nothing—being without love, hope, or life—was better than the torment of even the smallest affection.

The Call from Beyond the Abyss

Amid the utter darkness, something stirred—a gentle, almost imperceptible whisper telling me that I wasn't finished yet. I was at my lowest and most broken moment when I realized that even amid profound despair, there was a spark left within me. That spark was a reminder that I was more than the sum of my scars—a call to return to the love that had always been real, even when I couldn't see it.

It was in those abandoned moments that I found myself being led, step by tortured step, toward a light I had long forgotten existed. I was given one more child—a sign that echoed with the possibility of redemption. Amid the chaos of my life, there was an undeniable truth: I was not beyond hope. I needed to return to the only source of true, unfailing love—the love of God, made known to us through Jesus Christ.

A Glimpse of Divine Love and the Fruit of the Spirit

The turning point came when I allowed myself to embrace the only love that promises to last forever. It wasn't found in the arms of a person, but in the warmth of a Savior who had patiently waited for me all along. I found solace in the truth that goes beyond human faults.

"But the fruit of the Spirit is love, joy, peace, forbearance, kindness, goodness, faithfulness, gentleness, and self-control" (Galatians 5:22-23, KJV).

Those words were more than a verse on a page; they were a lifeline thrown to a drowning soul. As I turned my heart toward God, His love began to seep into the dark crevices of my brokenness. I started to understand that divine love wasn't about grand romantic gestures or fleeting passions of youth; it was about patience, kindness, and the audacity to believe in a better future, no matter how dark the present seemed.

In my struggle, I learned that true love has a transformative power. The very qualities that define the Fruit of the Spirit became my guide to spiritual growth and redemption. Gradually, the anger that had long characterized my interactions began to give way to a quiet gentleness. The bitterness I had sown for many years fell away, one act of forgiveness at a time. I started to nurture patience and forbearance, even when my heart longed for revenge in moments of profound hurt.

Embracing Self-Control: The Ultimate Expression of Love

Of all the fruits, self-control was the most difficult to grasp, yet the most liberating to live. Self-control wasn't about suppressing my feelings entirely but about choosing how I reacted to life's relentless challenges. It meant taking a deep breath instead of lashing out, pausing to reflect rather than reacting impulsively, and realizing that each moment was an opportunity to choose the love Christ showed me over the pain I once clung to.

Each morning, I wake up with the resolve to honor the gift of another day—to say, "Thank You, Lord, for your endless mercy and for gifting me a second chance." I meditate on the scriptures, nourishing my spirit with the truth that I am loved, not for what I have done, but because of who I am in Him.

Self-control keeps me anchored in the present, preventing me from falling back into old habits. It gives me the strength to resist the pull of familiar, destructive patterns. When anger rises, I remember that giving in would only dishonor the transformative love I have discovered. When I feel the desire to numb my emotions, I pause, pray, and choose healing instead of self-destruction.

In every trial and struggle, I see evidence of God's work within me. I notice it in the gradual change of my reactions and how I now choose forgiveness over resentment. Through His love, I regain control of my life and reclaim my story. I stand as a testament that even in the depths of darkness, there is light—

a light that encourages us to grow, to love, and to walk in true freedom.

Sharing My Story: A Beacon for Others

I share this testimony not to glorify the pain, but to give voice to the truth that those of us who are scarred by our past are not lost. I share to remind everyone who is hurting that the dark chapters of our lives do not have to define our future. They are stepping stones on a path that leads to real, sustaining love—a love that is patient, kind, and transformative.

For every person who has felt broken by the hands meant to protect, for every soul who has been abandoned or betrayed, know that you are not alone. I have walked that road, I have experienced that deep, consuming darkness, and I have emerged on the other side—albeit forever changed. There is power in the blood of Jesus. This serves as a reminder that He has endured, so we are healed, and that story is a testament to the fact that no matter how broken we feel, hope always remains.

The journey was not easy. There were days when the weight of my past nearly stole my breath, moments when I believed I would never see the light again. Yet, even then, a spark remained—a spark nurtured by God's unwavering promise that nothing can separate us from His love. That spark grew, slowly but surely, manifesting in acts of self-control, in moments of genuine forgiveness, and in the quiet resolve to choose Jesus each day.

The Continuing Journey

Today, my path is illuminated by the Fruit of the Spirit. I strive to live the love of Christ daily—not just in moments of joy, but also in times of hardship. I face challenges with a heart that has learned to bow. I choose self-control over impulsiveness, kindness over cruelty, and faith over despair.

My story is not one of immediate perfection. I still battle old demons, and there are moments when the darkness whispers its familiar refrain. But I now know that I have the tools to confront it, that through the love of God and the guidance of His Spirit, I can choose life over pain. I am a work in progress—a testimony in motion, continually evolving and growing.

To anyone reading this who feels bound by their painful past, I say, "Hold on. Your story is not over." The darkness you face today is not your destiny. There is a love far greater than the scars you bear, a love that produces the Fruit of the Spirit even in the hardest seasons. It is a love that calls you to a higher purpose—a purpose built on grace, self-control, and boundless hope.

I share my journey so that those walking in the shadows may see a glimmer of light through my testimony. I share it to remind you that no matter how deeply you've been scarred, you can be healed. No matter how heavy your burdens feel, there is strength in surrendering to the love that never fails.

In embracing that love, I have discovered my true self, not the broken person I once believed I was, but a beloved child of God, capable of immense compassion, resilience, and transformation. That love has redefined everything for me. It has taught me that forgiveness is not about forgetting but about choosing to live differently. It has also taught me that self-control is the highest form of respect, both for myself and for the divine promise of love that dwells within me every day.

A Final Word of Hope

This is my journey—from the pain of a broken beginning to the discovery of a love so profound that it transforms even the darkest moments into lessons of hope. I continue to live by the Fruit of the Spirit, nurturing self-control and allowing God's love to guide me through each new day. By sharing every raw and challenging part of my story, I hope you will find reflection, strength, and the courage to believe in the possibility of redemption.

Beyond every hurt lies the potential for healing, and within every scar lies the quiet beauty of survival. I stand here as living proof that love—true, redemptive, and enduring—can lead us out of darkness and into a life filled with purpose and grace.

You matter. Your pain does not define you. Your past does not bind you. There is always hope waiting in the light of God's love. Embrace the journey, trust in His promises, and know that you are never alone.

This is my truth—a journey through the shadows into the light, guided by love, strengthened by self-control, and continually nurtured by the Holy Spirit who never gives up on me. I share it with the fervent hope that anyone who feels lost or broken will see a spark of hope in these words and know that healing is possible.

Marlowe R. Scott

Dedication: To my blessed Christian family that I was born into. They demonstrated love, gentleness, and Christian values. Therefore, I can use my voice and talents to make a positive difference at home, in the church, and in the community.

Bio: Marlowe R. Scott has authored over a dozen books and submitted numerous stories for publication to Pearly Gates Publishing and Redemption's Story Publishing. She has penned stories in the Fruit of the Spirit series and the Spiritual Warfare series as well. Her awards have included being a #1 Bestseller, an International Bestseller, and a #1 Amazon Hot New Release. Marlowe is proud to say Angela R. Edwards is her daughter and a successful publisher of the two companies shared above. Additionally, Marlowe has received numerous awards for her handcrafted dolls, wreaths, floral arrangements, quilts, and other creations over the years.

Restraining and Gaining

Introduction

The Holy Bible contains many verses and life stories that emphasize the need for self-control, which countless men and women have used. The Fruit of the Spirit is listed in Galatians 5:22-23. The New International Version states it as follows:

"But the Fruit of the Spirit is love, joy, peace, forbearance, kindness, goodness, faithfulness, gentleness, and self-control. Against such things, there is no law."

A Bible concordance provides many scripture references, each intended to offer a better understanding of the verse. I often use a concordance to learn about instances in both the Old and New Testaments.

While everyone needs self-control in various settings, such as at home, church, and work, it significantly impacts how we are perceived. Reading the Bible, attending church, participating in Bible study, and becoming actively involved in a Christ-centered church can all help achieve self-control. A sincere person will search and read scripture such as Proverbs 25:28:

"A person without self-control is like a city with broken-down walls."

Having faced many disappointments, I often reflect on those times and realize that sometimes those experiences lasted for endless hours, days, months, or even years. I genuinely believe that God was with me throughout, even when I didn't see it at the time. As I grew older, reading the Bible, attending church, and participating in Sunday school strengthened my confidence in my spiritual path. A favorite childhood song I sing, especially during tough times, is "Jesus Loves Me!" I know I am part of God's spiritual family, and when I die, my soul will rejoice in Heaven.

The first word, "Restraining," in my story's title refers to God's way of limiting or holding back evil, sin, temptation, or the revelation of things that aren't needed at the moment we seek them. However, those things—jobs, places, relationships, etc.—may come later at the right time. My blessings come through practicing self-control, discipline, and prayer.

****
Whom Shall I Fear? – A Poem
Marlowe R. Scott © 2018

What can man do to me?
Harm my body? Yes.
Harm my soul? NO!
I AM God's child.
Angels protect my SOUL,
And because of that,
Heaven remains my GOAL.
In Heaven, I'll see Jesus—
My Master, Savior, and King.
I will have the peace and JOY
Only Heavenly realms can bring!
Promises will be fulfilled.
I will rest and shout, "HALLELUJAH!"
Jesus, the Lord, my Protector, I will see.
What can man do to me?"

****

There are times when we MUST walk away from situations that tempt us to become irritated and lose our self-control. I personally know women and men who stayed in unhealthy relationships that led to their health declining, with some reaching the point of death or taking their own lives.

Ephesians 6:12 (NIV) states, *"For our struggle is not against flesh and blood, but against the rulers, against the authorities, against the powers of this dark world, and against the spiritual forces of evil in the heavenly realms."*

As an adult, you might encounter some of the following situations:

➢ You might sometimes be ignored.
➢ False words may be spoken against you. Even family and close friends might be the ones spreading falsehoods.
➢ A common situation is when a family member or friend borrows money and doesn't repay you. Then, later, they might try to borrow again!
➢ Yet another challenge that really tests my family, coworkers, friends, and supervisors is those who nag about every little thing, not just the big issues.

I'm sure the list could be longer, but with self-control, we must find a way to manage and overcome each situation.

****

Restraining – A Poem
Marlowe R. Scott © 2025

Restraining from many of life's experiences
Is not always an easy, simple action.
Even an infant reacts when hungry by crying,
While an adult might use their mouth by loudly speaking out.
For those in school or at work, there might be biased words from others to take,
And often, responses, movements, or words we may loudly make.
Also, those working in large, diverse workforces
May have policies and rules that seem unfair—even prejudiced—
Resulting in many sleepless nights, ulcers, and a sharp tongue,
And clear unhappiness and poor work output start.
Many more examples can be given;
However, learning and using restraint with God's guidance,
You will surely be able to overcome.

****

　　To develop self-control, it is wise to start with small, manageable steps. Be patient as you build self-discipline, which requires time and effort. Visit churches to hear spiritual sermons. Feel free to join in singing, Bible studies, and more when you feel led to. Pray for spiritual comfort through the guidance of the Holy Spirit. Join a church for the right reasons, not just because family and friends are members. Have daily prayer and devotional time at home. Listen to Christian music and programs at home and while driving. For those with good voices, consider joining a choir. Get involved with church activities whenever possible, such as serving as a Sunday school teacher or a missionary.

During times of depression, mental anguish, and challenges, I sing songs to soothe myself. A short list includes:

➢ "I Want Jesus to Walk with Me."
➢ "I Got Joy, Joy, Joy Down in My Heart... Down in My Heart to Stay."
➢ "Real, Real, Jesus is Real to Me. Oh, Yes! He Gives Me Victory. I Can't Live Without Him... He's So Real to Me!"
➢ And my childhood favorite song: "Jesus Loves Me, This I Know. For the Bible Tells Me So. Little Ones to Him Belong. They Are Weak, but He is Strong. Yes, Jesus Loves Me. Yes, Jesus Loves Me. Yes, Jesus Loves Me, For the Bible Tells Me So."

Some suggestions to help you distance yourself from situations and people who insult and challenge you include:

➢ Say, "May the Lord bless you," then turn and walk away.
➢ If you're on the phone, say goodbye and end the call.
➢ If it's an organization, stop attending. It's not uncommon for church officers to resign. I also left a church when the Holy Spirit told me to leave.

"But I tell you, love your enemies and pray for those who persecute you" (Matthew 5:44, NIV).

****

Growing in Faith – A Poem
Marlowe R. Scott © 2015

Our spiritual gift of faith,
Like the small mustard seed,
Is planted by God and must grow
Into a deep-rooted belief
That our Heavenly Father nurtures
As the sun, winds, and
Storms of life come and go.
While our fruitful day may not readily come,
God continues the sunshine and rains
And counts each budding leaf one by one.
You see: He knows the end before we do
Because all His promises are definitely true,
And we must have faith to see the growing period through.
When we begin to mature and bear the fruit as we should,
We will see the positive outcome of those times we waited
And realize that our God surely has been more than good!

****

A few essential steps can help you restore your pride and self-respect, such as:

➢ Learn to discipline yourself by developing a consistent routine.
➢ Build positive habits.
➢ Minimize distractions and temptations.
➢ Learn to value your alone time, as family and friends may often interfere with your personal time.
➢ Begin with small steps where you can reduce distractions and tempting offers from family, friends, neighbors, and coworkers.

➢ For those seeking support online, BE CAREFUL about which organizations and professionals you listen to.

The following short list shares what the scriptures say concerning our spiritual walk and how relevant biblical times are to today's circumstances:

➢ Proverbs 16:9 – "In their hearts, humans plan their course, but the LORD establishes their steps."
➢ Proverbs 18:21 – "The tongue has the power of life and death, and those who love it will eat its fruit."
➢ Matthew 5:11 – "Blessed are you when people insult you, persecute you, and falsely say all kinds of evil against you because of Me."
➢ Matthew 6:33 – "But seek you first the kingdom of God and His righteousness, and all these things shall be added unto you."
➢ John 15:20 – "Remember what I told you: 'A servant is not greater than his master.' If they persecuted Me, they will persecute you also. If they obeyed My teaching, they will obey yours also."
➢ 1 Corinthians 6:19 – "Do you not know that your bodies are temples of the Holy Spirit, who is in you, whom you have received from God? You are not your own..."
➢ 1 Corinthians 10:13 – "No temptation has overtaken you except what is common to mankind. And God is faithful; He will not let you be tempted beyond what you can bear. But when you are tempted, He will also provide a way out so that you can endure it."
➢ Ephesians 5:18 – "Do not get drunk on wine, which leads to debauchery. Instead, be filled with the Spirit..."
➢ 1 Thessalonians 5:6 – "Therefore, let us not sleep, as do others, but let us watch and be sober."

- ➤ 1 Timothy 4:7 – "Have nothing to do with godless myths and old wives' tales; rather, train yourself to be godly."
- ➤ 2 Timothy 1:7 states it clearly – "For God has not given us a spirit of fear and timidity, but of power, love, and self-discipline."
- ➤ 2 Timothy 3:12 – "In fact, everyone who wants to live a godly life in Christ Jesus will be persecuted."
- ➤ Titus 2:2 – "Teach the older men to be temperate, worthy of respect, self-controlled, and sound in faith, in love, and in endurance."
- ➤ 1 John 2:16 – "For everything in the world—the lust of the flesh, the lust of the eyes, and the pride of life—comes not from the Father but from the world."
- ➤ Revelation 2:10 – "Do not be afraid of what you are about to suffer. I tell you, the devil will put some of you in prison to test you, and you will suffer persecution for ten days. Be faithful, even to the point of death, and I will give you life as your victor's crown."

Conclusion

Admittedly, practicing self-control can be challenging at times. Another term for it is "temperance," which refers to the ability to master emotions and practice moderation. The placement of SELF-CONTROL as the final Fruit of the Spirit holds significance. The first eight spiritual fruits—love, joy, peace, forbearance, kindness, goodness, faithfulness, and gentleness—are not always evident in every situation we face. However, by listening to sermons and studying the scriptures, we can learn the importance of each one. Yes, it may take time to learn and implement, but it is essential for all believers to practice each of the Fruits in their daily lives.

My prayer is that you've read something to uplift you and learned actions to implement with those around you. I leave you with the "Serenity Prayer":

God, grant me the **SERENITY** *to accept the things I cannot change, the* **COURAGE** *to change the things I can, and the* **WISDOM** *to know the difference.* (Written by Reinhold Niebuhr, Theologian, in 1932).

Maresa Roach

Dedication: This chapter is dedicated to the women who are battling self-control. *"For our struggle is not against flesh and blood, but against the rulers, against the authorities, against the powers of this dark world and against the spiritual forces of evil in the heavenly realms"* (Ephesians 6:12, NIV).

Bio: Maresa Roach is a daughter, sister, aunt, niece, and sister-girlfriend to many. She is a humanitarian who loves to serve communities, share her testimony, and evangelize to spread the Gospel of Jesus Christ wherever she goes. Her career and community service speak volumes as she acts as a change agent. She works as a Youth Engagement Specialist at Sasha Bruce Youthwork. Maresa has served seniors, volunteered for So Others May Eat (S.O.M.E.) and N Street Village Shelter for Women, and earned a service-learning trip to Cape Town, South Africa. Maresa is pursuing a Master of Social Work at Howard University. Connect with her on Facebook and Instagram @maresaroach.

Single, Saved, and Satisfied in Surrender!

Self-control—called "temperance" in the King James Version of the Holy Bible—is, of course, the ability to control (govern) oneself. It involves moderation, restraint, and the ability to say "no" to improper desires and fleshly lusts. Webster-Merriam defines self-control as "restraint exercised over one's own impulses, emotions, or desires."

The last characteristic of the Fruit of the Spirit listed in Galatians 5:22-23 is self-control. Each of the nine fruits—love, joy, peace, patience, kindness, goodness, faithfulness, gentleness, and self-control—represents changes to our character that result from the Holy Spirit's work in us. We do not become Christians on our own, and we cannot grow in faith by ourselves. Philippians 2:13 states, *"It is God who is at work in you, both to will and to work for His good pleasure."* Every good thing we do is the Fruit of the Spirit's work in our lives (gotquestions.org/fruitofthespirit).

I lost my virginity at age 15. It wasn't my plan to have sex with the person I entrusted with my purity, but it happened. I was coerced into thinking it would be okay. Call me naïve because that's what I was. I liked the boy and believed he liked me back. Later, I realized his goal was simply to sleep with me and move on. After losing my virginity, I think we slept together one more time before he started avoiding me. He got what he desired and no longer wanted anything to do with me.

That was the beginning of a cycle of allowing men to treat me as if I were unworthy and only a sexual object.

It was then that I realized I missed what I never had: a male figure—someone to love me. I started a pattern of dating men who didn't care for me and only wanted what they could get from me. I didn't have a father, and, as a result, my relationships with men reflected a search for love in all the wrong places.

I am also a survivor of sexual assault. Being violated is one thing, but being raped by several boys and men is another. That traumatic experience left me feeling alone, afraid, skeptical, and distrustful of people. Not just men, but people. (I have always been friendly and, at times, a bit naïve.)

After the rape, I became a promiscuous girl. Here is another situation where I trusted a guy who didn't have my best interests at heart. I liked the boy and went to his house to hang out with him. I didn't know where things would lead. I just wanted him to like me. When I arrived at his home, we started to kiss, and one thing led to another. Suddenly, he got off me, and out of nowhere, several boys and one older man appeared, forcing themselves on me. It's been so long ago that I don't remember exactly how many were involved. I know there were more than three. After that incident, I was in a state of shock. I can't even remember how I got home. It's all a blank. I was ashamed and felt it was my fault. I was violated but refused to tell anyone. The pain was deeply rooted in my body.

It took many years of disappointment and frustration before I realized that the men I dated didn't love me as much as I should have loved myself. I didn't feel fulfilled unless I had a man in my life. I was the type of woman who had to have someone lie beside me, despite how they treated me. I went from one failed relationship to another, shacking up with no fewer than four men in my life. It was a must that my man live with me or vice versa. If we weren't living together, we would spend most of our time at each other's homes. I "needed" a man's presence and love... by any means necessary.

I had no self-control! In fact, I was completely out of control! Out of control from the will of God—mentally, physically, and spiritually. I let my flesh dominate my mind, body, and soul because I enjoyed sexual immorality. At some point, it became a stronghold... one I no longer had control over.

You see, I became a victim of what I was victimized by. The one thing I didn't enjoy initially, I became addicted to. I couldn't get enough of sex, shacking up with a man, masturbation, and pornography. I yearned for the smell and taste of the sinful feelings, desires, and lust of the act I hadn't desired.

Abstinence seems to be a thing of the past for society. It can be hard to keep yourself to yourself when you've already stuck your hands in the cookie jar. "Keeping yourself to yourself" was something I learned at a young age. I was taught to save myself for marriage. Unfortunately, I didn't adhere to the rule. Instead, because of the negative sexual experiences I had, I let sin take control of my life.

Sex

"Marriage is honorable among all, and the bed is undefiled; but fornicators and adulterers God will judge" (Hebrews 13:4, NKJV). Sex should be reserved for a husband and a wife. As I mentioned, I was introduced to sex at a young age, which spiraled into a dangerous phase of indulging and not having control of the sexual acts I performed. I partly attribute my sex addiction to the rape. Oftentimes, people who've been victimized either fight or take flight. I chose neither. I simply

began to spiral out of control. I didn't particularly care for the path I was on, but I wanted to please the men I dated.

Fornication

"Flee fornication. Every sin that a man doeth is without the body; but he that committeth fornication sinneth against his own body. What? Know ye not that your body is the temple of the Holy Ghost, which is in you, which ye have of God, and ye are not your own? For ye are brought with a price: therefore, glorify God in your body, and in your spirit, which are God's" (1 Corinthians 6:18-20, KJV).

Masturbation

Let's be honest and clear here: Masturbation is an act of instant self-gratification. It is quite the opposite of self-control that is taught in the Holy Bible. Self-control is freedom from our passions and a gift from our Lord and Savior. This topic was a demonic stronghold for me. I would wake up thinking about sex and masturbate morning, noon, and night. It was such a daunting experience to crave the lasciviousness of the sin.

Pornography

There was a period in my life when I was addicted to watching pornography. What I know now is that all those sexually immoral feelings and habits were lying dormant in my spirit, caused by the soul ties I had with men from my past relationships. We don't always know who we are connected to when we sleep with others. Many are torn, bruised, and disdained by the iniquities of sin. It's no wonder I couldn't get enough of watching others commit acts of sexual immorality.

Perversion

After a period of grief and loss, I lost my ever-loving mind and turned to alcohol, sexual immorality, and swinger parties. Yes, I was introduced to swinger parties. I joined a group on social media and was "part of the club." I must say this: God had His hand on me. That period of my life was brief. I attended two parties and hung out with a few people, but I never became a serious swinger, poly, or any of the other terms a committed swinger would use. I was never meant to be part of that crowd. God broke that spirit of quick indulgence. It's a phase I am happy to testify I didn't dive deeply into.

Strongholds

In the realm of sexuality, strongholds manifest as persistent patterns of sexual sin, addiction, or distorted thinking that create barriers between believers and God. Scripture addresses sexual immorality extensively, with 1 Corinthians 6:18-20 instructing believers to *"flee from sexual immorality"* and to recognize that *"your bodies are temples of the Holy Spirit."* The Bible offers numerous examples of sexual strongholds—ranging from David's adultery with Bathsheba (2 Samuel 11) to the sexual immorality troubling the Corinthian church. However, the Bible also provides hope for freedom. The way to break strongholds involves confession, repentance, and the renewal process described in Ephesians 4:22-24: *"...putting off your old self... being made new in the attitude of our minds... putting on the new self."*

Surrendered to Jesus Christ

In 2019, the person I was dating broke up with me. I was depressed, distressed, and brokenhearted. I felt utterly alone.

During that time of despair, a friend invited me to her church. I was a wreck and unsure of what direction I was headed, but I knew I needed to surrender the pain to God. That Saturday, I'd been up all night, drinking. I thought drinking the pain away was the cure. My friend called me and asked if I was still coming to church, adding that the van would pick me up in the morning. I answered hesitantly, "Yes, but I am not sure if I have anything to wear." That Sunday, I went to church and enjoyed the word of God. When the altar call came and the pastor asked, "Are you saved? Do you want to rededicate your life to Christ? Do you need a church home?" I chose two of the three. I rededicated myself to Jesus Christ and joined the church... with a hangover. That day, I chose God, holiness, sanctification, and a lifelong commitment to Jesus Christ and purity to please God, not man.

It's been five years since I committed to abstaining from sex, and I trust in the promises of God. I have no desire to displease Him. Do I have feelings when I've wanted to masturbate? Yes. Have I had those feelings since I've been saved? Yes. I even tried a few times and honestly felt the urge, but God made it uncomfortable to pursue. To be transparent, only once did the enemy think he had me completely after I gave in to the desire. You see, masturbation opens portals to sin. It is a spirit, one that I cannot feed. Since then, I have not engaged in the act again, and I pray to God I never will. I have God's self-control fruit within me because I chose to follow Him.

Today, I am a healthy 58-year-old woman who desires a husband. God knows the desires of our hearts. I believe and have decided to surrender everything to God, and abstaining from sex is necessary. Initially, it wasn't easy, but I prayed and asked God to give me a pure heart that is acceptable to Him. As a Single, Saved, and Satisfied woman of God, I am in Full Surrender!

Walking in Freedom

The journey from bondage to freedom is rarely a straight path. Like footprints in the sand, sometimes washed away by waves of temptation, my steps toward wholeness have been preserved by grace alone. These five years of abstinence stand as a testament not to my strength, but to God's faithfulness when I finally surrendered everything—my broken past, my desperate need for validation, and my distorted understanding of intimacy.

In those quiet moments when loneliness whispers its familiar song, I remember that I am never truly alone. The same God who saw me at my lowest—drinking to numb the pain, searching for love in empty embraces, trapped in cycles of shame—is the same One who celebrates my victory today. He didn't just break my chains; He showed me they were never meant to define me.

To anyone struggling under the weight of sexual sin or trauma: your story isn't over. The same God who rescued me can restore you. Your previous mistakes, violations against you, and deepest shame cannot outmatch His redemptive power. Your body, mind, and spirit were created for something much more beautiful than what the world offers—they were made for a sacred purpose and holy pleasure within God's perfect boundaries.

The fields of grace and mercy are, indeed, in bloom. I am learning every day to walk through them with wonder, gratitude, and the Fruit of Self-control that comes not from striving, but from abiding in Jesus Christ.

Tiffany Pope

Dedication: This is dedicated to the people who call me Mama and Pooh-Pooh: We have so much to learn, grow, and do in this life together. I pray for our unity to be strong, beautiful, healthy, and unbreakable. Mama loves you, and God loves us all.

Bio: Tiffany Pope, affectionately known as "Sunnie," is a daughter and servant of the Most High, a mother, and a grandmother. On her journey to find purpose in life, she studied to become an LCDC, which led to her current role that allows her to combine her lifelong love for writing with helping others in a meaningful way by building a collegiate recovery community, renewing her sense of purpose, and fostering a closer walk with God. She loves farmhouse DIY crafting and has recently developed a passion for gardening to grow her own food for better health and wellness.

How Chaos Developed Discipline

"Like a city whose walls are broken through, is a person who lacks self-control" (Proverbs 25:28).

Leading up to my 9th-grade year, I had to take a summer school class. We had more fun than the law allowed. I was so excited to be a high schooler that you couldn't tell me a thing! Then, in one fell swoop, that excitement was washed away by the devastating news that my mother had brain cancer. That diagnosis shook my entire family to the core.

It all happened so quickly. It seemed like one minute she was climbing the corporate ladder, taking classes for certifications, and making better life choices. She had tried to quit smoking several times before, but this time felt different. This time, she held firm, and, after over 30 years of smoking cigarettes, she quit cold turkey but endured severe withdrawal. The weeks afterward were tough, but luckily, she had some help because around that time, cessation gums and patches became more readily available. Still, she experienced withdrawal symptoms like sweating, sickness, and irritability—the whole ugly mess. But through it all, she persevered. Everything seemed to settle down over time, and she started feeling better, one day at a time.

Then, one strange day, she didn't feel well. That morning, I went to my summer school classes, while my Mama stayed home from work in her pajamas and robe, which was very unusual for her. That day, she just sat on the couch, hardly moving around the house. Her condition continued to worsen. She had trouble talking and lifting her arm, so my dad decided we needed to take her to the emergency room. We hoped it wasn't related to the withdrawal, but unfortunately, it was much worse. She was actually having a stroke. We found out my Mama had a brain tumor, which was likely the cause of many problems she'd been trying to address for a while, like constant headaches and other issues she visited the doctor for.

And just like that, my high school life was about to become interesting in ways I never could have imagined.

Fast forward to graduation...

Mama fought through years of doctors' appointments, hopes deferred, and dreams no longer within reach. But when that day arrived, she got up, we got dressed, we laughed, we cried, and she made it to my graduation! She was so happy for me! And I was thrilled that she was there, as much on her feet as she could be after the multiple rounds of chemotherapy and radiation had all but killed her. Her hair was gone, her teeth had fallen out, and she was weak most days, yet she still could throw a punch like Muhammad Ali.

A little over a year later, the cancer came back, but more aggressively. We were told the tumor was the size of a grapefruit. By that time, Mama had already made it very clear that she would not be undergoing any more treatments because they were too hard on her, and whatever life she had left to live, she would do so on her own terms.

My Mama, Lila Marie Pope, passed away in May of 1998. Earlier that year, I found out I was pregnant with my first son.

Watching my mother battle a long-term illness took a heavy toll on me in ways I'm only now beginning to understand fully. I can still feel that wild, tumbling sensation in my body. Nothing was the same. Everything was gone. Everybody was still there but felt absent (if that makes any sense). Life definitely took some sharp turns on two wheels during that time. Being young, naïve, and not recognizing my fears caused chaos. I was like a city with its walls knocked completely down—defenseless and unprotected. I lacked the foundational wisdom of discipline.

Self-control is a gift with many benefits. It's one of God's ways of protecting us spiritually, mentally, emotionally, physically, and even financially.

A few years ago, at a previous job, we were planning a lesson for our group that week on the nine Fruit of the Spirit. I remember being really excited because I had just gotten more familiar with Galatians 5 during my own study time. As we kept discussing it throughout the week, I found something interesting in how Paul listed the Fruit of the Spirit that caught my eye. I noticed he named love first and self-control last. I started to wonder why that was important, knowing he was a very deliberate writer. It made me think of the roof and the foundation of a house.

I saw love as the roof—the covering of every house, the overhead protection. In 1 John 4:8, it is written that God is love. 1 Peter 4:8 affirms that love covers a multitude of sins. Additionally, 1 Corinthians 13:13 says, *"So now faith, hope, and love abide, these three; but the greatest of these is love."* That illustrates how God covers us with Himself. I'm so grateful that His love sustains me, even in the midst of my sins, and that no matter what I do, I cannot be separated from his love (Romans 8:39).

Then, I made a significant connection: self-control equals discipline—the foundation of life. Having a child is an enormous responsibility that should never be taken lightly. When they say, "Life is in your hands," that's as literal as it gets. We are shaped by every experience we have. Each one offers lessons and room for growth. I had to examine the shape of my life and determine what kind of foundation I was building on. Who was the common denominator? Who was making all the decisions that resulted in the total sum of me?

The math was simple: Me.

Not my parents. Not my siblings. Not my ex-husband or his family. Not my teachers. Not my pastors. Not my children. It's me. I am solely responsible for the choices I make in my life. What I say, what I eat, how I care for my body, my home, my finances, where I go, and how I treat others all fall under the self-control umbrella.

The intricacies of how God designed everything to work together are melodic. When we lack harmony in our lives, we can often identify where we haven't exercised enough self-control. We may have let our thoughts drift into negative spaces. Perhaps we didn't establish clear boundaries in certain relationships. We negotiated with the enemy instead of saying no. Those moments transform us, either for better or worse, but make no mistake: they will definitely change you.

Setting boundaries with myself was the starting point. I needed to rely on myself first before I could be truly accountable to others—and that's a messy and chaotic place to be, especially in your early 40s with a family depending on you to keep your promises, all while trying to be that for yourself. I've looked deeply in the mirror, prayed long prayers, and had honest conversations with God, and I'm making progress. Even when I miss the mark and don't quite hit my goals, I stay encouraged.

The beauty lies in the daily effort I invest in myself, in the ongoing process of bringing my flesh into submission.

What I've come to realize is that self-awareness is a major key factor in having self-control. It's the foundation on which the other fruit are built. I had to exercise self-control to receive God's love, which includes His disciplinary actions, and to understand that He chastens me because of His love for me (Hebrews 12)—not the opposite—because He desires for me to share in His holiness.

When we have self-control, we can build our lives with joy, access God's peace, and be patient with ourselves and others. Find constant ways to show kindness to others. Practicing self-control naturally brings out the goodness God has placed in all of us. We must remain faithful to God to access any of His fruit. I believe gentleness comes from being in God's presence through prayer and bringing our issues to Him. All of these require the strength that comes from having discipline within us.

Looking back at how I handled life after losing my mother, I see clearly how I didn't understand self-control from a biblical point of view. Honestly, I didn't really know the Bible well at that time. I made many mistakes by living according to my flesh. I lacked true knowledge of discipline and what it meant to control myself, my thoughts, my emotions, and my body.

After I gave birth to my son, I got married a year later, but it was too soon. I moved away from my family and thought I would be okay, but I soon realized I needed them. I had no direction in life, no fundamental understanding of the Word of God. I flopped, floundered, flipped, and ran in circles for a very long time, but through His Word and every one of His kept promises, I am better—we are better, solid, and thriving.

All the while, God kept me. All glory belongs to Him.

Let us pray...

Lord, I thank You for the Fruit of the Spirit. I thank You for covering our lives with You and Your love, and for protecting us at all times, keeping us close to You when we were brokenhearted. I thank You for bringing Your Word into clear view to give us a deeper understanding and enrich our lives. We love You and cannot say Thank You enough.

Thank You for this opportunity to pour out my heart and share my story with others. I pray, Lord, that it resonates deeply with each person and that Your Word is forever pressed into their hearts so they will hunger to work on their discipline and continue to cultivate Your fruit in the garden of their souls.

We praise You and sing, "Glory! Hallelujah to Your name!"

In Jesus' name, we pray all these things and so much more. Amen.

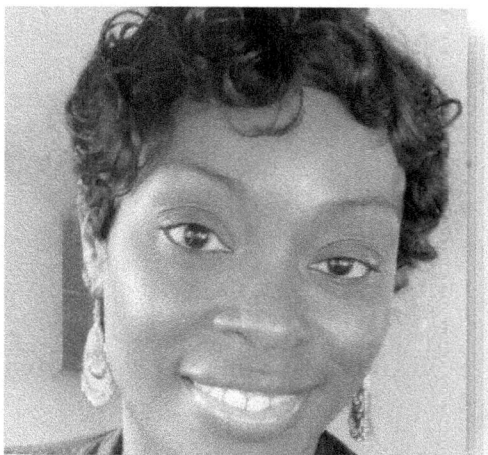

Dr. Sonya Alise McKinzie

Dedication: To my daughter, my heart and greatest gift: Your light inspires every word I write and every life I touch. To every woman rising from pain to purpose, may you find healing, hope, and the courage to build your legacy. This is for you. Keep thriving. Keep believing. Keep becoming.

Bio: Dr. Sonya Alise McKinzie, the 2025 American Mother of the Year, is a trauma recovery coach, founder of ThriveHER Inc., and author of 24 impactful books—both co-authored and independently written. A survivor-turned-advocate, she empowers women to heal, grow, and build lasting legacies through faith and resilience. Her transformative work uplifts communities and inspires women to reclaim their voices and walk boldly in purpose. Above all, Sonya is the devoted mother of a 14-year-old daughter—her greatest joy and most prized possession—embodying the heart of her mission to nurture, lead, and thrive. Connect with her at www.thriveher.me.

Cultivating the Spirit in the Heat of Co-Parenting

Fruits in the Fire

When I was 18 years old, I received a diagnosis that would quietly shape the next three decades of my life: Polycystic Ovary Syndrome, or PCOS. The doctor's words were clinical, but their weight was crushing: "The likelihood of you having children is slim." At that age, I was barely an adult, still learning how to navigate life, yet suddenly, I was being told that motherhood—a dream I hadn't even fully formed—might never be mine. I remember sitting in that sterile room, the hum of fluorescent lights above me, trying to process what felt like a life sentence. It was a grief I didn't know how to name.

As the years passed and I entered my thirties, I began to make peace with the idea of infertility. I told myself that maybe motherhood wasn't meant for me. I buried the ache deep within, masking it with ambition, education, and career goals. But even as I tried to move forward, there was a quiet longing that never fully left me. I had accepted what the world said was true about my body, but God had a different narrative.

At 34, something miraculous happened. I found myself staring at a pregnancy test, then another, and another one, confirming what I could hardly believe: I was pregnant. At 35, I gave birth to my daughter, my miracle. It was a divine contradiction to every medical report I had ever received. I was a single mother, yes, but I was a mother. And that truth was both beautiful and terrifying.

I remember the fear that gripped me in those early days. I delayed telling the father of my child because I already knew his stance: he didn't want another child. When I finally shared the news, his reaction was exactly what I expected: disbelief, anger, and accusations. He believed I had deceived him, that I had somehow orchestrated this miracle as a trap. But how could I explain that this child was not the result of manipulation, but of divine intervention? That God had opened a womb the world had labeled barren?

Despite the tension, I chose to embrace my pregnancy with joy. I relied heavily on my faith and the unwavering support of my mother. I was working full-time, pursuing a master's degree, and navigating pregnancy alone. It was among one of the most challenging seasons of my life, but also one of the most blessed. I clung to the promise of Romans 8:28:

"And we know that in all things, God works for the good of those who love Him, who have been called according to His purpose."

After giving birth, the real battle began. Co-parenting wasn't a shared journey; it was a battlefield. The father of my child would come and go, appearing for months only to disappear again, each time leaving emotional wreckage in his wake. There were court visits—eighteen in total over 14 years—each one a reminder of the fractured relationship and the toll it was taking on our daughter. Child support battles, visitation modifications, unnecessary welfare checks—it felt like we were constantly under siege.

There were days I felt like I was losing my mind. The weight of single motherhood, emotional manipulation, and the legal stress were all too much. Defiantly, I questioned God. *"Why would You bless me with this miracle, only to surround it with so much pain? Why couldn't her father and I co-parent in peace? Why did my daughter have to witness so much conflict?"* In those moments, I was reminded of Galatians 5:22-23:

"But the fruit of the Spirit is love, joy, peace, forbearance, kindness, goodness, faithfulness, gentleness, and self-control. Against such things, there is no law."

I clung to those words like a lifeline. I prayed for patience when I wanted to scream. I prayed for self-control when I wanted to retaliate. I prayed for peace when chaos seemed to be our constant companion.

Therapy became a necessity for both my daughter and me. We needed help processing the trauma, instability, and emotional whiplash. We also leaned into prayer, surrounding ourselves with a community of believers who interceded when we were too weary to pray for ourselves. There were nights when I cried myself to sleep, feeling completely alone, depleted of faith, and drowning in despair. I hid my pain from the world, wearing a mask of strength while crumbling inside.

And then, in 2025, something shifted. The father of my child decided to step away... again. Our daughter, now a teenager, expressed her desire to no longer be caught in the crossfire. She wanted peace. She wanted to feel joy again. And for the first time in years, we had it. It wasn't the outcome I had prayed for, but it was the answer I needed. The silence that followed his departure was not empty; it was sacred. It was healing.

Looking back, I see how God used every trial to shape me. The years of conflict, tears, and courtroom battles were all part of the refining fire. James 1:2-4 says, *"Consider it pure joy, my brothers and sisters, whenever you face trials of many kinds, because you know that the testing of your faith produces perseverance. Let perseverance finish its work so that you may be mature and complete, not lacking anything."* I didn't understand it then, but I do now. The fire wasn't meant to destroy; it was meant to cultivate fruit.

I learned patience, not during calm moments, but in the storm. I learned self-control, not when things were easy, but when I wanted to lash out and chose silence instead. I learned to trust God, not when I had answers, but when I only had questions. And I learned that peace is not the absence of conflict, but the presence of God during it.

Although it has only been a few months since the other parent chose to walk away again, my daughter is stronger and wiser beyond her years because of what she has endured. She has seen the cost of resilience, the power of prayer, and the beauty of grace. Yes, we carry scars, but they are not wounds; they are testimonies. We are proof that God can bring life from barrenness, peace from chaos, and joy from sorrow.

This chapter of our lives—this long, winding, painful, beautiful chapter—is what I call "Fruits in the Fire." It is the story of how God cultivated the Spirit within me through the heat of co-parenting. It is a story of redemption, of growth, and of grace. And it is a reminder that even when the world says "no," God's "yes" is louder.

So, to every mother walking through the fire, to every woman told her womb is barren, to every parent fighting for peace—hold on. God is not finished. The fruit is coming. And when it does, you will see that every tear, every prayer, and every sleepless night was not in vain.

"Let us not become weary in doing good, for at the proper time, we will reap a harvest if we do not give up" (Galatians 6:9).

****

Harvesting Peace: Guided Lessons in Patience from the Co-Parenting Journey

1. **Trust God's Timing:** At 18, I was told I might never have children due to PCOS. I grieved silently for years, but God had a different plan. At 35, I gave birth to my daughter—a miracle that defied medical expectations. *"For nothing will be impossible with God"* (Luke 1:37).

2. **Embrace the Unexpected with Faith:** Becoming a single mother wasn't the path I envisioned, but I leaned on Romans 8:28 and trusted that God was working all things for good— even the hard things.

3. **Anchor Yourself in Prayer and Scripture:** When co-parenting became a battlefield, I turned to God's Word. Galatians 5:22-23 reminded me to cultivate the fruits of the Spirit—especially patience and self-control.

4. **Set Boundaries and Protect Your Peace:** Years of legal battles, emotional manipulation, and instability taught me the importance of boundaries. Peace became a priority, not a luxury. *"If it is possible, as far as it depends on you, live at peace with everyone"* (Romans 12:18).

5. **Seek Support and Healing:** Therapy and prayer warriors helped my daughter and me process the trauma. Healing came through community, counseling, and consistent prayer.

6. **Forgive Daily, Even Without Apology:** Forgiveness was a daily choice. I released bitterness not for the other parent's sake, but for my own freedom. *"Forgive as the Lord forgave you"* (Colossians 3:13)

7. Celebrate the Small Victories: Every peaceful exchange, every moment of joy, every court resolution—I celebrated them as signs of God's faithfulness.

8. Let God Refine You Through the Fire: The trials didn't break me—they refined me. James 1:2-4 taught me that perseverance through trials leads to maturity and completeness.

9. Speak Life Over Your Child: Despite the chaos, I spoke blessings and truth over my daughter. She grew up knowing her worth, her strength, and her identity in Christ.

10. Rest in God's Peace: In 2025, the conflict ceased. It wasn't the ending I prayed for, but it was the peace we needed. God had cultivated ***Fruits in the Fire.***

Dr. Cheryl Kehl

Dedication: To every woman who has ever felt pulled in a thousand directions but still longs to honor God with her time— this chapter is for you. I pray you find freedom in living by Heaven's clock and courage to walk in purpose, one faithful hour at a time.

Bio: Dr. Cheryl Kehl is a dynamic author, minister, business strategist, and faith-based family coach committed to empowering women, strengthening families, and fostering generational healing through Christ-centered values. She hosts the Christian TV talk show Walking in Greatness, where she inspires audiences to embrace their God-given purpose and overcome life's challenges. As a certified Christian life, intimacy, and relationship coach, Cheryl equips women to heal from domestic violence, restore boundaries, and build thriving families. With degrees in Business and a Doctorate in Biblical Studies, she champions resilience, reconciliation, and transformation—helping others turn pain into purpose and walk boldly in greatness.

Time Management as a Spiritual Discipline

For many years, I believed that productivity was the primary goal of time management. I focused heavily on meeting deadlines, checking things off my lists, and trying to impress ministry leaders and corporate America supervisors. However, I eventually realized that being busy doesn't necessarily mean being productive. Being busy can deplete you, while being fruitful can bring a sense of satisfaction. The truth is: we can only be truly fruitful when our time aligns with our divinely mandated purpose.

"Teach us to number our days, that we may gain a heart of wisdom," says Psalm 90:12. That verse is more than just a reminder to stay organized. It urges us to live intentionally with eternity in mind. I recall a time in my life when I was doing all the "right" things, such as volunteering at church, arriving early for meetings, and accepting every request made of me. I appeared trustworthy and well-behaved on the outside but felt tired and unfulfilled inside.

One morning, as I was praying, the Lord whispered, "You are managing tasks, but you are not stewarding your calling." I was completely stunned by that statement. That was when I realized that time management is both a spiritual discipline as well as a tool for success. From then on, I learned to see my schedule as an altar where I can glorify God rather than just a planner to be filled. (That will be a significant part of my life if I can master it.)

Seeing Time the Way God Sees It

To embrace time as a spiritual discipline, we must view it from God's perspective. In the Bible, time is described in two ways:

- Chronos—the routine passage of minutes, hours, and days—is the first. We use clocks and calendars to keep track of this type of time.
- Kairos—those special times when Heaven and earth meet that are predetermined by God—is the second.

Both are necessary for a wise existence. To be mindful of the passing of Chronos, we are urged to count our days. However, we are also called to identify and seize Kairos—divine opportunities that may appear insignificant at first glance but have everlasting significance. Maintaining a schedule is only one aspect of true time management. Another part is living with awareness of God's will.

Romans 12:1 instructs us to "present our bodies and lives as a living sacrifice, holy and pleasing to God." That includes our schedules. When we order our days according to God's priorities, we are making a declaration of worship:

"LORD, MY TIME BELONGS TO YOU."

Why So Many of Us Struggle with Time

You're not alone if you've ever felt like there's never enough time in the day. Managing your time isn't just about getting things done; it's also about how you feel. Often, poor time management indicates larger issues. Sometimes, it's because you don't know what truly matters in the moment, so everything seems important. Other times, it's overcommitment driven by the desire to make others happy or avoid letting them down. (Overcommitment has always been one of my biggest problems.) For many of us, it's because our phones and screens prevent us from being purposeful. And sometimes, it's because we avoid dealing with what's going on inside by staying busy on purpose.

Until those deeper roots are addressed, no planner or productivity system will truly succeed. Sometimes, the very idea of "balance" increases the pressure, or just thinking about "balance" makes things worse.

People talk about "work-life balance" as if life were a scale that could always be evenly weighted. But life has its ups and downs. There are times when work demands more from us, and other times when family, health, or ministry must take priority. The idea isn't strict balance but harmony—a rhythm that reflects what God wants you to do right now.

Creating a Life Around What Matters

So, what is it like to use time management as a spiritual practice? I have discovered four key concepts that help me stay focused:

- First, consider why you're doing it. Before writing down your tasks or filling out your schedule, pause and reflect on what God has entrusted to you for this season. Ask questions like, "Who am I supposed to help right now?" and "What actions genuinely help me reach the goals God has set?" By answering those questions, you find ways to prioritize your commitments. Not every invitation is worth accepting. I had to learn to say no more often to grow in this area.

- Second, establish rhythms instead of imposing strict restrictions. We often discuss this at work by emphasizing the importance of healthy rhythms. God designated the pattern from the beginning: six days of work and one day of rest. That rhythm wasn't just practical; it was deeply spiritual. We can also create rhythms in our personal lives. Allocate time for focused work, genuine rest, the people who matter most, and both spiritual and professional growth. These rhythms provide stability, creating space for growth and development. Since I work for a church, maintaining healthy rhythms is essential for me. It's easy to become overwhelmed with ministry work, which can disrupt our sense of harmony.

- Third, learn how to differentiate. Not every good opportunity is from God. I learned the hard way that saying yes to too many things because they seemed valuable was a mistake. Wisdom asks, "Will this help me get closer to my goal or pull me away from it?" Prayerful discernment protects us from distractions masquerading as opportunities. We also need to discern whether it will draw us away from God and His true calling for our lives.

- Finally, leave some space in your schedule. Our culture promotes hustling, yet the Bible instructs us to make room. We show our faith in God when we set aside time for breaks, interruptions, and divine appointments. I find myself in the most trouble when my schedule is completely full and God sends someone I need to minister to. We are saying, "Lord, I don't have to fill every moment to prove my worth. I have faith that You will make my work more effective."

Some Practical Ways to Steward Time Well

These concepts only matter if you put them into practice every day. Over the years, I've learned a few simple things that help me stay aligned with my mission. One of them is my morning alignment routine. I spend time with God—reading the Bible, praying, and listening—before I pick up my phone or check my email. Then, I ask the Lord one simple question: What is most important today? I use that answer to help create my to-do list. If my schedule is too packed, it becomes harder to do that.

Another strategy is to focus on three major wins each day. We start all our meetings and huddles at church by sharing wins. This is an essential habit for me, as it gives me something to share. I create a list of three key things that matter most to me, rather than a long list of duties. If I complete those, I can relax at the end of the day. It clarifies things and prevents me from getting lost in the urgent while neglecting the vital. Am I a pro at this? Not yet, but it is what I strive to make a regular practice every day.

My boss has trained us to use time blocking. Assigning a specific amount of time to each activity helps me stay focused and resist the urge to say, "I'll get to it later." The decision is made in advance once the time is set. Next is the Sabbath. I set aside work for one day a week, not just to take a break, but also as an act of faith and obedience. It reminds me every week that my worth isn't based on how much I do, and that God sustains me.

And finally, digital boundaries. Technology is useful, but it also consumes our time. I occasionally check my Facebook usage and am surprised by how much time I spend there. When

I'm focused on work, I try to keep my phone out of reach. I struggle to concentrate on multiple things at once. I rarely turn off my ringer, but I keep my phone on silent so I don't hear new notifications. For some people with sick parents or small children, disconnecting to that extent can be difficult.

The Emotional Battles Around Time

Even with those habits, managing time can be hard on your emotions. Taking a break can sometimes make you feel guilty. Many of us—especially women—think that "taking it easy" makes us lazy, but taking a break isn't a sign of weakness; it's a sign of obedience. Jesus took a break from the crowds to pray and rest.

Another struggle is the fear of missing out. You can say "no" confidently when you live according to what God wants for you. You won't miss what you never had.

There is also perfectionism, which is the idea that if something isn't flawless, it's not worth finishing. However, perfectionism can slow down progress. Sometimes, it's better to be good and done than perfect and late. (This is important for me to remind myself constantly.)

Conclusion: Living by Heaven's Clock

As a spiritual practice, managing our time changes how we live. It transforms a calendar into a canvas on which God paints His plans. When we approach each hour with purpose and obedience, it becomes an offering. This isn't about doing more; it's about doing what matters most. It's about making sure our hours align with what Heaven wants us to do so that our lives are not just full but also useful. And when we live this way, our legacy is more than what we accomplished; it's the story of a life well-lived, one hour at a time.

Questions for Reflection

1. Do you see more busyness or more productivity in your current schedule? Why?
2. Which things in your life right now align with God's calling, and which ones feel more like distractions?
3. What do you do that makes it difficult for you to manage your time? Do you overcommit, get distracted, avoid tasks, or try to be perfect?
4. What would it be like for you to create rhythms instead of seeking balance this season?
5. Which truth from this chapter would set you free the most if you could truly accept it?

Afterword

As we conclude this deep exploration of self-control, it becomes clear that this virtue is much more than just discipline—it's a dynamic, life-affirming force that shapes our spiritual journey and personal growth. The stories and reflections shared throughout this collection highlight the complex nature of self-control as both a divine gift and a human effort, closely linked with faith, resilience, and love.

The main message from these stories is that self-control isn't about being perfect or denying yourself, but about intentionally living in line with God's will. It takes courage to face difficult truths, honesty in relationships, and humility to seek God's guidance each day. Whether dealing with addiction, trauma, relationship struggles, or life's responsibilities, self-control shines as a source of hope and a way to heal. It helps people break harmful cycles, set healthy boundaries, and find peace amid life's storms.

The biblical foundations and personal testimonies underscore that self-control is closely linked to other Fruits of the Spirit—love, joy, peace, patience, kindness, goodness, faithfulness, and gentleness. Together, these virtues form a complete framework for spiritual growth and emotional health. The document's focus on self-control as the final fruit encourages readers to view it as the stabilizing force that maintains balance among the others, supporting a life that honors God and nurtures the soul.

Reflecting on these findings, it is evident that self-control is essential in trauma recovery, addiction treatment, and emotional regulation. The experiences of contributors show that developing self-control can turn even the darkest moments into stories of redemption and grace. This underscores the importance of further research into how spiritual disciplines like self-control can be incorporated into therapy and community support to promote complete healing.

Furthermore, practical insights on time management, boundary setting, and emotional regulation highlight promising paths for creating resources and programs that help individuals live Spirit-led lives. Future research could also explore the cultural, psychological, and social factors affecting the practice of self-control, expanding understanding of how this fruit appears across different contexts.

Ultimately, this collection conveys a powerful message: self-control is a journey, not a destination. It is developed moment by moment, choice by choice, through God's grace and the strength of the Spirit. It encourages us to embrace our humanity with compassion while pursuing the divine goal of mastery over ourselves. As we continue to walk through the fields of grace and mercy, may we carry forward the lessons learned here—living intentionally, speaking truth, and nurturing the fruit that leads to freedom, peace, and an abundant life.

May this work inspire ongoing reflection, dialogue, and growth, encouraging all who read it to pursue self-control as a sacred discipline that transforms lives and communities alike.

Self-Control—It's in God's Word

1. Galatians 5:22-23

"But the fruit of the Spirit is love, joy, peace, forbearance, kindness, goodness, faithfulness, gentleness, and self-control. Against such things there is no law."

This passage lists self-control as a Fruit of the Spirit, highlighting it as a divine gift essential for living a Spirit-led life and growing in holiness.

2. 2 Timothy 1:7

"For the Spirit God gave us does not make us timid, but gives us power, love and self-discipline."

Self-control is presented here as self-discipline, empowered by God's Spirit, enabling believers to overcome fear and live boldly.

3. Proverbs 25:28

"Like a city whose walls are broken through is a person who lacks self-control."

This metaphor emphasizes that without self-control, a person is vulnerable to harm and chaos, underscoring its importance for personal stability.

4. 1 Corinthians 9:25

"Everyone who competes in the games goes into strict training. They do it to get a crown that will not last, but we do it to get a crown that will last forever."

Paul compares self-control to an athlete's discipline, illustrating that spiritual growth requires intentional effort and restraint.

5. Titus 2:11-12

"For the grace of God has appeared that offers salvation to all people. It teaches us to say 'No' to ungodliness and worldly passions, and to live self-controlled, upright and godly lives in this present age."

Grace enables believers to practice self-control, rejecting sinful desires and living in a way that honors God.

6. Proverbs 16:32

"Better a patient person than a warrior, one with self-control than one who takes a city."

This verse values self-control and patience above external victories, highlighting its power in personal character and relationships.

7. James 1:19-20

"My dear brothers and sisters, take note of this: Everyone should be quick to listen, slow to speak and slow to become angry, because human anger does not produce the righteousness that God desires."

Self-control is essential in managing emotions, especially anger, to live righteously.

8. 1 Peter 5:8-9

"Be alert and of sober mind. Your enemy the devil prowls around like a roaring lion looking for someone to devour. Resist him, standing firm in the faith..."

Maintaining self-control is part of spiritual vigilance, resisting temptation and standing strong in faith.

9. Romans 12:2

"Do not conform to the pattern of this world, but be transformed by the renewing of your mind. Then you will be able to test and approve what God's will is—his good, pleasing and perfect will."

Self-control is involved in resisting worldly influences and renewing the mind to discern God's will.

10. 1 Thessalonians 5:6

"So then, let us not be like others, who are asleep, but let us be awake and sober."

Sobriety here implies self-control in thought and action, encouraging believers to live alert and disciplined lives.